MORALITY AND CAPITALISM

MORALITY AND CAPITALISM

A Dialogue on Freedom

David L. Kendall

Copyright © 2015 David L. Kendall

All rights reserved. Printed in the United States of America. No part of this book may be reproduced in any manner whatsoever without written permission except in the case of brief quotations embodied in critical articles and reviews. For information, address David L. Kendall, 824 Birdie Dr., Abingdon, VA 24211

ISBN-10: 1503233243
ISBN-13: 9781503233249

Dedicated to

Laura Ann, my loving and beautiful wife, who has endured listening to me think out loud about many of the ideas in this book, well beyond the point of distraction, but who loves me anyway.

And Jessica, my artful and talented daughter, who told me I should write a book.

Acknowledgments

Nothing is more rare than an original idea. After at least 40 years of reading and hearing the ideas of hundreds of brilliant people, it is quite impossible for me to know whose ideas I have long ago adopted as if they were my own. If ever I had an original idea, I cannot tell you for sure what it is. Contrary to the hopes of academicians everywhere, I think that we who scribble a few words together in an essay may be unwitting plagiarists, regardless of how many citations we offer up. The list of philosophers, economists, scientists, novelists, and countless other scholars, who through their words or writing planted ideas in my mind, is by now quite long and utterly irretrievable.

Still, I must name a few who shaped many of the ideas readers find in this book. In my undergraduate days, Paul Heyne's textbook, *The Economic Way of Thinking*, illuminated light bulbs in my mind on nearly every page.[14] I believe professor Heyne's book taught me foundations of just about all that I take myself to know about economics. A few years later in graduate school, the ideas of Milton Friedman had strong and lasting influence, with *Free to Choose*[15] and *Capitalism and Freedom*[16] forging permanent ideas in my mind about human dignity, liberty, and capitalism. Years beyond graduate school, Deidre McCloskey's book, *The Rhetoric of Economics*,[17] convinced me that economics and philosophy have a large, unavoidable intersection.

Like most other people, I take myself to be a good person. But I had never really thought seriously about morality until I read and listened to the ideas of Peter Kreeft.[18,19] Professor Kreeft got me started; now, no end is in sight; so much to read, so little time. The literature of moral philosophy is vast, and as Robert Heinlein's protagonist Valentine Michael Smith said, "I am only an egg."[20]

I am honored by and grateful to the University of Virginia's College at Wise, whose faculty and administration granted me a sabbatical leave in spring 2012 to work on this book. I am also grateful to the five students, Tim Bush, Barklie Estes, Daniel Jones, Ethan Lavallee, and Joel Sprinkle, who took my honors course in fall 2011, titled "The Morality of Capitalism." Their questions, comments, and objections helped shape this book. I am also especially grateful to Candaş Kirnaz, my Turkish friend and former student, who is the inspiration for my fictional interlocutor, Tyro.

Finally, and significantly, I thank my true friend, my *telia philia*, Bobby Miser, who has done his best to teach me about asking and believing.

Table of Contents

	Part I: Morality	xiv
Chapter 1	What Is Morality?	1
	Threesville	3
	The Fundamental Hypothesis of Economics	5
	The Golden Rule	9
	Kant's Categorical Imperative	11
	The Moral Imperative	13
Chapter 2	Human Nature	18
	What We Want	19
	What We Value	23
	How We Choose	27
Chapter 3	How We Know What Is Moral	35
	How We Know Anything	35
	Justification from Emotion	49
	Justification from Reason	50
Chapter 4	Can the Moral Imperative Work?	56
	The Moral Imperative in Everyday Life	57
	The Moral Imperative and Moral Dilemmas	64
Chapter 5	Why Be Moral?	68
	Morality and Reciprocity	69
	Morality and Virtue	70
	Morality and Freedom	74
	Morality and Social Cooperation	75

	Part II: Capitalism · 80
Chapter 6	What Is Capitalism? · 81
	Private Property · 82
	Voluntary Exchange · 95
	Freedom · 105
	Law · 106
	Is Capitalism Moral? · 110
Chapter 7	What Capitalism Is Not · 111
	Why Is Capitalism So Reviled? · · · · · · · · · · · · · · · · · · · 111
	Democratic Cronyism · 114
Chapter 8	Morality, Capitalism, and the Good Society · · · · · · · · · · 120
	The Good Society · 120
	Life Without Capitalism · 123
	Life With Capitalism · 127
	Can We Get There From Here? · · · · · · · · · · · · · · · · · · · 138
	References and Notes · 143
	About the Author · 161

Preface

Most people want to be good people, and most people are. In *How to Win Friends and Influence People,* Dale Carnegie recounted stories of how even America's most notorious criminals, men like Al Capone and Two Gun Crowley, didn't see themselves as bad people.[1] Even Hitler did not see himself as a bad guy. People want to be good, and they want to be thought to be good by others. For that reason, morality matters to people, because we cannot be good people if we are not first moral people.

This book is not about *how* capitalism works to advance human prosperity, which it surely does. This book is about the moral foundations of capitalism. Tens, if not hundreds, of excellent books have explained how capitalism works. The writings of Adam Smith,[2] Frederic Bastiat,[3] Ludwig von Mises,[4] Ayn Rand,[5] Milton Friedman,[6] Friedrich Hayek,[7] Israel Kirzner,[8] George Reisman,[9] and Murray Rothbard[10] are but a few exceptional examples. A complete list of authors who have explained more than ably how capitalism generates human prosperity would run to tens of pages.

History shows unequivocally that capitalism works to generate widespread prosperity for humans. That conclusion is no longer much debated.[11,12] Capitalism definitely works. Yet, for all its success in generating human prosperity, capitalism is reviled by hundreds of millions of people around the globe. Googling the phrase "capitalism images," yields anecdotal evidence of how reviled capitalism is. The search produces a panoply of images that convey negative, evil, or diabolical meanings for capitalism, with scarcely a positive, good, or inspiring image to be found. Why? Why is capitalism so denigrated?

Faced with undeniable historical evidence that capitalism generates unmatched prosperity for humans, its opponents have retrenched. Now the critics of capitalism claim that it is unjust, un-green, and immoral—never mind that it works. The mantras of "social justice," "save the planet" and "we're all in this together" have replaced the soundly debunked Marxist claim that socialism would inevitably be the bright future of humans.[13] If you like capitalism, say its critics, shame on you. Now, the enemies of capitalism exhort us to support a democratic socialist agenda—because democratic socialism is "just," "green," and "egalitarian," say the critics of capitalism.

Is capitalism unjust? Are contemporary opponents of capitalism right, claiming as they do that capitalism is immoral? That is the question this book explores. Because people want to be moral, the undeniable historical evidence that capitalism generates widespread prosperity is simply insufficient to silence the critics. For indeed, *if capitalism is immoral*, it should be rejected.

Part I: Morality

Do you not see, first, that—as a mental abstract—physical force is directly opposed to morality; and secondly, that it practically drives out of existence the moral forces?

AUBERON HERBERT [21]

1

What Is Morality?

I had taken a course in Ethics. I read a thick textbook, heard the class discussions and came out of it saying I hadn't learned a thing I didn't know before about morals and what is right or wrong in human conduct.

CARL SANDBURG[22]

Solon: Why so glum, Tyro?

Tyro: Someone stole my iPod.

Solon: How do you know? Maybe you just misplaced it.

Tyro: No, I didn't misplace it. I left it on the hood of my car in the parking lot at school this morning, while I was loading up my backpack. I know it's dumb, but I forgot to pick it up. I remembered it by the time I got to my first class, but when I got back to my car, it was gone. I'm really bummed.

Solon: Maybe one of your friends picked it up; maybe you will get it back.

Tyro: I wish I could believe that.

Solon: Well, what would you have done if you had seen an iPod sitting on the hood of someone's car?

Tyro: I guess I would have picked it up, if I knew whose car it was.
Solon: What if you did not know whose car it was?
Tyro: I guess I'd still have picked it up.
Solon: To turn in to the Dean's office?
Tyro: Sure. If I kept it, that would be stealing.
Solon: So, what is wrong with stealing?
Tyro: Everyone knows that; stealing is just wrong.

—⁂—

Moral behavior is *right* conduct for humans when they interact with other humans. Moreover, morality is a prescriptive code that all rational people agree governs the behavior of all other rational people, and the behavior of any other rational life forms, if any exist. Whether humans are the only creatures on earth who are rational remains an open question.[23] If some other life forms on earth are also rational, then we humans are obligated to interact morally with them also.

Humans may be the only rational beings who live on earth, but they are certainly not the only sentient beings. Sentient beings are those capable of feeling and perhaps are conscious of themselves, even if they are not rational.[24] Many people believe that humans are obligated to interact morally with all sentient beings, not just other humans; others disagree, and still others are uncertain. If people are obligated to interact morally with *all* sentient beings, the implications are certainly profound, but beyond the purposes of this book, which focus on human interaction.

Stealing is a particular kind of immoral human conduct, which is to say that stealing is *wrong* conduct for humans. All rational people—from all cultures, times, and places—know that stealing is wrong conduct for humans; moreover, all rational people agree that they should not steal. Even thieves know stealing is wrong, and they agree they know it is wrong. We humans also know that murder, rape, battery, enslavement, and fraud are wrong conduct for humans. And we all know that we know. The author N. Kenneth Rideout calls it *The Truth You Know You Know*.[25]

THREESVILLE

"Threesville" is a fictional society comprising just three people: Annie, Bobby, and Callie. We can use the ultra-small society of Threesville to explore moral, political, and economic questions. Considering questions about morality and the political economy in such a small society promotes great clarity. And as it happens, what we find true in Threesville we also find true in societies of most any size.

The citizens of Threesville reside together on a remote island isolated from other people. Its three citizens produce all the goods and services in Threesville. With only three citizens, Threesville does not use the social institution of money; all economic interactions occur by barter. Thinking about economics with money removed also promotes great clarity. The three citizens of Threesville are not family members; hence, they have no familial obligations to one another; the three are independent, rational individuals.

Annie is a smart, self-motivated, and talented woman. She is decisive, a natural leader, and physically attractive. Annie has the highest annual income and greatest wealth of all three citizens of Threesville (Annie's income is goods and services she produces; remember, Threesville does not use the social institution of money). She is an accomplished person who works hard, but she has also been lucky in life. Annie owns a lot of land in Threesville, some of which she acquired by homesteading, but some of which she acquired by purchase from Bobby and Callie several years ago. Annie lives well, but she also saves some of what she produces, thereby accumulating capital. She has an eye to the future, but doesn't neglect enjoying the present.

Bobby is an intelligent, fun loving, life loving guy who has great understanding of human nature. He is neither handsome nor plain; he is pleasingly manly. Annie and Callie like Bobby, for he is unusually likeable. He is a natural, in just about every sense of the word. He's authentic. He's just fun to be around. When he laughs, which is often, Annie and Callie can't help laughing, too. And of course, like most people with such attributes, he does quite well in life. Though not as wealthy as Annie, he's no pauper. Bobby doesn't worry much about the future; he believes the future will be just fine.

Callie is not particularly intelligent, not particularly confident, and not particularly talented. She also hasn't been particularly lucky in life. Callie is rather ordinary in appearance. She works hard, but the work does not pay well (which is to say, Callie does not produce much in the way of valuable goods and services). Callie is the "poor" one in Threesville, living pretty much from hand-to-mouth, as they say. Years ago, Callie sold most of the land she owned to Annie. Callie sold her land (which is to say, she exchanged her land for other goods and services produced by Annie), because Annie offered a really high price, which Callie was quite happy to get. Callie worries a bit about the future, but she believes she has no means to prepare for it, so why worry too much?

With Threesville formally introduced, let's use it. Morality has meaning in Threesville, but morality would have no meaning whatsoever in Onesville, because "moral conduct" is the answer to the question "what is right conduct for humans interacting in a social context?" Without at least one other rational being in the picture, the concept of morality is empty and meaningless. If Bobby and Callie were not around, Annie would be free to behave any way she chooses. After all, if Annie were the only rational being in her world, who would care how Annie behaves but Annie?

As noted already, some people believe that other beings who are sentient but not rational would care. But again, for purposes of this book, we shall sidestep that thorny and important issue, focusing instead only on the interaction of humans.

THE FUNDAMENTAL HYPOTHESIS OF ECONOMICS

Most people behave morally most of the time. But immoral behavior gets most of the attention, which tends to distort our perception of human behavior. If all rational people know the moral law, agree that they should behave morally, and want to be moral people, why do some people sometimes behave immorally?

Tyro: Do you think that every person who has ever lived has stolen something?

Solon: I do not doubt it.

Tyro: But doesn't everyone know that stealing is wrong?

Solon: I think everyone who has ever stolen anything knew it was wrong.

Tyro: Then why did they steal?

Solon: Why did *you* steal?

Tyro: Who said I stole something?

Solon: Did you?

Tyro: (looking a bit sheepish) Yes. Did you?

Solon: (also looking a bit sheepish) Yes. Plato thought that people do what they believe is wrong due to a kind of ignorance. He thought that if people knew—really knew—what is good for them, they would do only what is good for them.

Tyro: That sounds a little like something my economics teacher told us. He called it the "Fundamental Hypothesis of Economics." According to the FHE, "people choose those actions they believe will yield them their greatest value."

Solon: I think the FHE, as you call it, and what Plato thought are very much related ideas, although neither Plato nor any other ancient Greek philosopher thought much about economics.

Tyro: So, if people steal, they somehow think the outcome will be good for them, even though they believe stealing is wrong?

Solon: Plato's explanation seems reasonable. How else can we explain immoral behavior?

Tyro: Maybe it is just human nature for people to behave immorally. Maybe people behave morally only if they fear being punished.

Solon: Some philosophers have made that argument, Thomas Hobbes for one. Do you refrain from stealing only because you fear being caught and punished?

Tyro: No. I know stealing is wrong. I don't steal because I don't want to be a bad person.

Solon: Plato would have liked your reason for not stealing, Tyro. I think Plato is right. Thieves do not know—really know—that stealing is bad for them. I think Plato believed that stealing, like other immoral acts, damages the soul.

Tyro: I don't think anyone ever stole something from me before, Solon. Now that I have experienced it personally, I will certainly never steal again.

Solon: I am pleased to hear that, Tyro. But what if you were starving and had no food. Would you steal another person's food?

Tyro: (after a long silence) If I were starving and I did steal food, would that really be immoral?

Solon: What do you think, Tyro?

Tyro: I've never experienced being hungry with no food around, so I can't say for sure, but I think I would steal food to stay alive. Would that really be wrong?

Solon: That depends on what we mean by "wrong."

Tyro: "Wrong" means "not right."

Solon: And "right"? What does "right" mean?

Tyro: (hesitating) I don't know just how to say what "right" means. But I can give examples of what wrong behavior is. Stealing is wrong. Murder is wrong. Rape is wrong. Battery is wrong. Fraud is wrong. Lying is wrong.

Solon: What is wrong with stealing, to repeat a question I asked you earlier?

Tyro: Stealing is wrong because it makes me feel angry and unhappy if someone steals from me.

Solon: I do not think your feeling angry and unhappy makes stealing wrong. Is it not the other way around? Stealing makes you angry and unhappy because it is wrong. What is it about someone stealing your iPod that makes you angry and unhappy?

Tyro: I'm not sure.

Solon: What in life makes you angriest of all, if it happens to you? I do not mean a particular event; I mean a kind of event.

Tyro: (with some passion) It's the same thing that makes anyone angriest of all. I can't stand to be forced to do something.

Solon: Just so, Tyro! No one wants to be forced—to be compelled—by another person.

Tyro: (now excited) I get it! Stealing makes me angry because the thief is compelling me to give up my property. No one has the right to do that. Stealing is wrong because stealing is compelling another person.

Solon: Tyro, I believe you have identified the very core of "wrong" human conduct, the very meaning of immorality.

As Tyro says, stealing is compelling others to give up their property. And so it goes with all other immoral behaviors. Murder is compelling another to give up one's most valuable property of all, life itself. Rape is obviously compelling another. Battery is obviously compelling another. Enslaving someone is obviously compelling another. Lying with intent to defraud, which we will call guile, is compelling another, although less obvious than direct physical force.

Solon: Did you get your iPod back, Tyro?
Tyro: (with a scowl on his face) No. I'm kicking myself for leaving it on the hood of my car the other day, and I'm wishing I could kick whoever stole it.
Solon: So, you blame whoever took it?
Tyro: Wouldn't you?
Solon: Yes, if I knew the thief were a rational person.
Tyro: Stealing is wrong and everyone knows it. What does rational have to do with it?
Solon: Suppose a squirrel carried off your iPod. Would you blame the squirrel?
Tyro: Are you serious?
Solon: Entirely.
Tyro: What do you mean by "rational person"?
Solon: By "rational person" I mean beings, such as humans, who are able to reason, and are therefore able to know some statements are true by thinking alone, and who are able to know that they know, and who are able to choose their actions based on logical reasons, reasons of which they are aware.
Tyro: I see what you mean. I would be upset if a squirrel took my iPod, but I couldn't really blame a squirrel. I doubt if squirrels know right from wrong.
Solon: Just so, Tyro. I, too, doubt that squirrels are rational creatures. If they are not, the moral law that binds rational beings does not apply to squirrels. By virtue of their irrationality, squirrels are unfit to be bound by the moral law.
Tyro: I think that whoever stole my iPod knew that stealing is wrong.
Solon: I do not doubt it.

The behavior of beings who are not rational is strictly amoral. Rationality is a necessary condition for a being to be bound by the moral law. Intentionality is also a necessary condition for an act to be immoral. If Bobby runs over Annie with his car unintentionally, Bobby's act is not immoral, although it may have been negligent. Intentional acts of rational people that compel others unjustly are immoral. All other acts are moral.

THE GOLDEN RULE

The literature of moral philosophy and religion is vast. Countless authors, philosophers, theologians, essayists, playwrights, and novelists have written millions of words about moral conduct. Googling the word "ethics" or the word "morality" yields about 49 million results each. Near the top of each list of results, one finds hyperlinks to articles that contain hyperlinks or references to every imaginable treatise, ancient and modern, on morality and ethics. A fascinating web site called *Project Gutenberg* provides free access via the Internet to thousands of classic texts on moral philosophy.[26] With only modest effort, countless hours of reading serious dissertation about moral philosophy are but a few mouse clicks away from anyone with access to the Internet. Yet, after all the words, after all the scholarly treatises, after all the esoteric distinctions, morality comes down to a single, simple imperative—*do not compel unjustly*—which we may call the Moral Imperative.

Can the moral law really be that simple? What about the Golden Rule? It would be difficult if not impossible to name a religion or ethical code that does not propose some form of the Golden Rule as the overarching moral law.[27]

HINDUISM (C. THIRTEENTH CENTURY B.C.)

Do not to others what ye do not wish done to yourself . . . This is the whole Dharma. Heed it well.—The Mahabharata

JUDAISM (C. THIRTEENTH CENTURY B.C.)
    What is hateful to you, do not do to your neighbor; that is the entire Torah; the rest is commentary; go learn it.—The Babylonian Talmud

ZOROASTRIANISM (C. TWELFTH CENTURY B.C.)
    Human nature is good only when it does not do unto another whatever is not good for its own self.—The Dadistan-i-Dinik

BUDDHISM (C. SIXTH CENTURY B.C.)
    Hurt not others in ways that you yourself would find hurtful.—The Tibetan Dhammapada

CONFUCIANISM (C. SIXTH CENTURY B.C.)
    Do not do to others what you do not want done to yourself.—Confucius, Analects

CHRISTIANITY (C. FIRST CENTURY A.D)
    Therefore all things whatsoever would that men should do to you, do ye even so to them—Matthew 7:12, Luke 6:31

ISLAM (C. SEVENTH CENTURY A.D.)
    No one of you is a believer until you desire for another that which you desire for yourself.—"The Sunnah," from The Hadith

BAHÁ'Í (C. NINETEENTH CENTURY A.D.)
    Ascribe not to any soul that which thou wouldst not have ascribed to thee, and say not that which thou doest not. This is my command unto thee, do thou observe it.—Bahá'u'lláh, The Hidden Words

The Golden Rule is an ancient idea found in all cultures and times, which should not surprise us, since the rule accords entirely with our own individual experience and reasoning about *right* human conduct. But the Golden Rule may be too permissive. For example, the Golden Rule seems to permit a masochist to inflict pain on someone who is not a masochist. The Irish dramatist and co-founder of the London School of Economics, George Bernard Shaw, said, "Do *not* do unto others as you would that they should do unto you. Their tastes may not be the same."[28] The Golden Rule may also be an impractical prescription for human behavior, since we frequently do not know how others want to be treated. Funny thing about human minds; one's own mind is completely available to one's self and completely unavailable to anyone else.

KANT'S CATEGORICAL IMPERATIVE

Kant's Categorical Imperative is arguably the most influential statement of moral philosophy, aside from the Golden Rule. The two statements Kant proposed as expressions of what he took to be a single Categorical Imperative are abstract and brilliant, if a bit obscure:

> *Act only according to that maxim by which you can at the same time will that it should become a universal law.*
>
> *Act so that you treat humanity, whether in your own person or in that of another, always as an end and never as a means only.*[29]

Kant's moral philosophy argues that morality must be universal, reciprocal, and intentional acts of individual good will. We are not to act in ways that we do not want every other person to act. We are not to claim rights to behavior for ourselves that we do not grant to others. Moral behavior is willed behavior. For Kant, moral behavior is right behavior, not because of its consequences, but entirely because moral behavior is the act of a good will.

Many people agree with Immanuel Kant, who proposed that moral behavior is an absolute obligation—a duty of humans—which is to say that morality is deontological (from the Greek *deon*, "obligation, duty"; and *–logia*, "sayings").[30,31] Deontological morality isn't situational, circumstantial, utilitarian, or relative. We are obligated to behave morally all the time, not just on Tuesdays. We are obligated to behave morally even when we are starving, not just when we are not. Morality isn't about the greatest good for the greatest number. Good ends do not justify immoral means, notwithstanding the utilitarian theories of Jeremy Bentham and John Stuart Mill.[32] Means are part of ends, if the means involve force, threat of force, or guile. For Kant, and many other philosophers, morality is in no way relative; we are *absolutely* obligated to other human beings to behave morally.

To some, Kant's Categorical Imperative seems to be little more than an abstract, somewhat obscure re-statement of the more ancient Golden Rule. Of course, Kant did not think so. He thought his Categorical Imperative overcomes certain defects that keep the Golden Rule from being a complete statement of morality. For example, a criminal would like to be shown mercy from a judge. The Golden Rule seems to say that a judge would act morally by absolving the criminal. But Kant's Categorical Imperative rules out such absolution, because we would not want *all* crimes to be absolved, even though criminals would like the idea.

Tyro: Surely the Golden Rule and Kant's Categorical Imperative are solid moral philosophies, no?

Solon: Of course, Tyro. The Golden Rule is sometimes called the "ethic of reciprocity." The Principle of Reciprocity is how we know by reason alone what is moral. If I would steal from you, I grant to you the right to steal from me. If I would murder you, I grant to you the right to murder me. Kant's Categorical Imperative is mostly a restatement of the Golden Rule and it's underlying Principle of Reciprocity, esoteric fine points aside. The Golden Rule and Kant's Categorical Imperative are definitely touchstones of moral philosophy. But both may be impractical, too permissive, and too abstract to serve as a moral compass for all people. Still, neither the Golden Rule nor Kant's Categorical Imperative deserve much criticism

---

THE MORAL IMPERATIVE

The moral law can be stated simply and plainly in terms that all rational people understand. Believe it or not, some people do not completely understand what Kant said about morality. Fortunately, the moral law can be stated in just four words—*do not compel unjustly*—which we will call the Moral Imperative. Immoral human conduct is behavior that intentionally compels another rational being unjustly. Moral conduct is any behavior that does not compel unjustly.

The Moral Imperative is entirely consonant with the Golden Rule, but it is simple, clear, concise, and concrete. The Moral Imperative is also consonant with Kant's Categorical Imperative. But everyone understands the Moral Imperative and every rational person agrees that the Moral Imperative is right conduct for humans. Moreover, all rational people know that they know the Moral Imperative is right conduct for humans.

Tyro: The Moral Imperative says, "do not intentionally compel unjustly." But what does "unjustly" mean? Doesn't the adverb "unjustly" make the Moral Imperative ambiguous?

Solon: An excellent question, Tyro! What do you think the word "unjustly" means?

Tyro: Let's find out. Here in the *Online Etymology Dictionary* for the word "just" it says: "late 14c., 'righteous in the eyes of God; upright, equitable, impartial; justifiable, reasonable,' from O.Fr. juste 'just, righteous; sincere' (12c.), from L. iustus 'upright, equitable,' from ius 'right,' especially 'legal right, law'."[33]

Solon: Certainly helpful information, Tyro. Again, what do you think the word "just" means?

Tyro: Well, since I don't know much about the "eyes of God," I will avoid that potential meaning. I am drawn more to the words "justifiable," "reasonable," and "right."

Solon: As you should be, Tyro. If an act is "justifiable" that means it is "reasonable," which means the actor has "right reasons" for actions. "Just" acts are those done for right reasons. "Unjust" acts are those done for wrong reasons.

Tyro: So, compelling another person for wrong reasons is compelling unjustly?

Solon: Just so, Tyro. Compelling another for right reasons is not immoral.

Tyro: Can we always know if our reasons are right reasons?

Solon: We can if we are rational. The Principle of Reciprocity and logic guide us.

Tyro: Do you think that two rational people will always agree about whether some act of compulsion is just or unjust?

Solon: "Always" is a strong word, Tyro. Perhaps "usually" or "probably" are more apt.

Can we dismiss claims that morality is situational, relative, or even meaningless, as some say?[34] We can. Can we dismiss the Golden Rule and Kant's Categorical Imperative, replacing them with a single, four-word moral law, the Moral Imperative—*do not compel unjustly*? We certainly should not dismiss the Golden Rule, nor Kant's Categorical Imperative, but we can state the moral law simply, clearly, concisely, and concretely with the Moral Imperative alone.

The Moral Imperative does not leave much to the imagination. The Moral Imperative is deontological; it is absolute, consistent, and logical; it is in no way situational, relative, or meaningless. The Moral Imperative is a statement of the moral law that all cultures in all times agree is right human conduct. Moreover, all cultures in all times agree that the Moral Imperative is a moral law that *should* govern the behavior of all people. No other moral philosophy is as ubiquitous among all people of all cultures and times.

Tyro: Somehow, the condition of "justice" in the Moral Imperative is still troubling to me, Solon. Can the Moral Imperative be an absolute moral law if we must decide when compulsion is "just"?

Solon: The idea of justice cannot be avoided, Tyro. Bear in mind that the Moral Imperative does not mean "justice" as an immutable, ultimate value that exists in the realm of Plato's ideal forms, or somehow otherwise outside human thinking. Justice also does not mean "fair," as it did for John Rawls.[35] Nor does justice mean "deserved," as it did for Robert Nozick.[36] For the Moral Imperative, "justice" means right reason.

Tyro: But how can we know what is a "right reason"?

Solon: It's what humans do, Tyro. Humans are rational beings. If we cannot know right reason by thinking alone, we simply cannot know it.

Tyro: You asked me before if I would steal food to stay alive. What if I did steal the food of another, but stealing was the only way I could stay alive? What if the person I stole from had plenty of food? By stealing food, I would certainly be compelling. But would stealing to stay alive be immoral? Would I be compelling another person unjustly?

Solon: Stealing is immoral, regardless of the reason one may have for stealing. Virtuous ends do not justify immoral means. Morality is not about consequences of actions; morality is about actions themselves. In any case, why would you steal? Asking someone for food is not shameful. Most people are more than willing to give some of their food to another person who is hungry. You could ask others for food instead of stealing from them.

Tyro: What do you mean by virtue, Solon?

Solon: Let us say that virtuous behavior is good behavior, a praiseworthy habit of choice. That definition will do for now.

Tyro: Aren't morality and virtue really the same thing? Lots of people seem to think so.

Solon: Morality and virtue are not the same thing, notwithstanding what your dictionary or thesaurus may say. Moral behavior is a necessary condition, but not a sufficient condition for virtuous behavior. We cannot be virtuous if we are not first moral, but we could be moral without being noticeably virtuous. People behave morally or they do not; no shades of gray. Morality is zero-one; on or off; yes or no. But people may be more or less virtuous; virtue admits to degrees. Callie may be more virtuous than Bobby, even though both always behave morally. Annie cannot be more moral than Callie, but both can behave morally without a bit of virtuous behavior from either.

Tyro: What if a starving person asks others for food, but others will not share their food. Would stealing food still be immoral?

Solon: You have already said that if you steal food owned by another person, you would be intentionally compelling that person for your own gain, subverting the will of another human being for your own benefit, did you not?

Tyro: Yes, but it seems to me that stealing food to stay alive would be an exception. Why would that kind of compulsion be unjust?

Solon: You have asked an important question, Tyro, so let us consider it carefully. If you compel another person, you do three things at once: you assert that your own ontological value is greater than that of the person you compel; you deny the will and choice of another rational person, substituting your own will and choice for the other's; and most important, you sacrifice your own right to be free of unjust compulsion by others. By your compulsion of another person, you grant other people the right to compel you—by the Principle of Reciprocity. As Aesop put it, one who steals has no right to complain if he is robbed.[37].

Tyro: What do you mean by "ontological value"?

Solon: Ontology is the philosophical study of "being"— that which is. By ontological value, I mean the value of a person simply as a being—as a soul—or a mind if you prefer. Not value for what the person knows, has done, or might do; just value as a living, rational being alone.

Tyro: It seems to me that each person has the same ontological value.

Solon: Indeed, Tyro. We have no reason to think otherwise. Equal ontological value is precisely what people have in mind with the idea of all people having equal rights. People believe they have the same rights as any other human. But we all have but one right, and we have it because we are ontologically equal. We each have the right not to be compelled unjustly by another. For anyone to have that right, every person must also have a responsibility—a duty, as Kant puts it. Each of us has the duty not to compel others. If we ignore our duty—denying the right of another to be free of compulsion—we instantly undermine our own right to be free of compulsion. Again, that idea is the Principle of Reciprocity.

Tyro: So, stealing is immoral, no matter what the reason?

Solon: I think so; what do you think?

Tyro: I think I have much to think about.

> *[Handwritten note:]* what determines when compelling is unjust?
>
> *[Handwritten note:]* stealing from people who "stole" from you

2

Human Nature

Know thyself

PAUSANIAS[38]

The kind of behavior that is right for humans will depend on the kind of beings we humans are—on our human nature. As St. Thomas Aquinas proposed, if our nature were different, our duties would be different.[39] We humans are obligated by our nature to behave morally. Our rationality and ability to know are the two foundational elements of human nature that make us fit for the moral law. Within these two foundational properties of human nature lie three interconnected elements of our nature that make morality possible—what we want, what we value, and how we choose.

Solon: Good morning, Tyro. And what a beautiful morning it is.
Tyro: (a bit dejected) I've seen better.
Solon: Really? What is wrong with this day? What more could you want?
Tyro: I don't think it's a beautiful day. The sky is overcast and the forecast is calling for rain. I wanted to play golf today.
Solon: Why did you want to play golf?

Tyro: I like golf; it's fun.
Solon: Why do you want to have fun?
Tyro: Because I feel good when I'm having fun.
Solon: Why do you like to feel good?
Tyro: Everyone likes to feel good.
Solon: Why does everyone like to feel good?
Tyro: Why are you asking "why" over and over again, Solon?
Solon: To find out what it is that you really want. If you knew what you really want, maybe you would not mind so much if it rains today.
Tyro: Why didn't you just say so? That's easy; I really want what everyone wants; I want to be happy.

WHAT WE WANT

> *Happiness is that state of consciousness which proceeds from the achievement of one's values.*
>
> AYN RAND[40]

In his landmark book, *Human Action,* Ludwig von Mises wrote, "Human action is purposeful action."[41] Long before the time of Mises, St. Thomas Aquinas wrote in *Summa Theologica*

> *All things contained in a genus are derived from the principle of that genus. Now the end is the principle in human operations, as the Philosopher states (Phys. ii, 9). Therefore it belongs to man to do everything for an end.*[42]

Aquinas reserved the title "the Philosopher" for Aristotle alone, who wrote *The Physics* in 350 BCE, which Aquinas references. The idea that we humans act by choice and for purpose is truly ancient. But even if that idea were not ancient, we all believe it is true by our own experience and reason. *Pursuit of Happiness...*

The end toward which all human action aims is happiness. In *Nicomachean Ethics*, Aristotle called it "*eudaimonia*" (from the Greek *eu*, "good" and *daimōn*, "spirit"), commonly translated as "happiness."[43] Professor Daniel Robinson proposes that a more apt rendering for the word might be "flourishing."[44] We humans agree, pretty much unanimously, that happiness or *eudaimonia* is what we all want, even though we do not all agree about how to achieve it.

If we ask people what they want in life, the final answer typically ends up being happiness. All the other things we want are means to the end of happiness, not ends in themselves, just as Aristotle said. All that we do in life, all that we want in life, all that we hope for in life—all are only means to an end—to be *eudaimon*.

Like Aristotle, we all agree that wanting to be happy is fundamentally part of our human nature; we all want to flourish, thrive, be content, and succeed in life. If we asked people why they want to be happy, all we would get is puzzled looks, for we have reached the end of the line. No explanation for wanting to be happy makes any sense to us, nor should it. *Eudaimonia* is the greatest good, the *summum bonum*, for humans; wanting to be happy seems to be part of what it means to be human. Plato thought virtue is the *summum bonum* for humans, but Plato and Aristotle were not at odds, for neither thought we humans can achieve *eudaimonia* if we are not first virtuous. But we cannot be virtuous if we are not first moral.

Being *eudaimon* does not mean having a continuous psychological state of joy and merriment, although joy and merriment are certainly welcome. People want to flourish, to thrive, to be good at living—all dimensions of *eudaimonia*. And as Aristotle also noted, people want to avoid misery, even though some suffering will likely be part of flourishing. As Rabbi Abraham Heschel put it, the man who has not suffered—what does he know anyway?[45] According to Aristotle, one becomes *eudaimon* by virtuous action in accord with reason.⁴⁶ A necessary condition for being *eudaimon* is to be good at being human. Being good at being human requires being good at what is *essentially* human; namely, being rational.

Solon: Can you not be happy today without playing golf, Tyro?

Tyro: I can't think of anything else that would make me happier today.

Solon: What if someone returned your stolen iPod. Would that not make you happy?

Tyro: Yes, that would make me happy, because my iPod was valuable; I've been upset ever since someone stole it.

Solon: Why do you say your iPod was valuable?

Tyro: It cost me a lot of money, money that I can't afford to lose.

Solon: What if someone had given you the iPod instead of you spending your money to buy it?

Tyro: An iPod is valuable whether someone gives it to you or you buy it yourself.

Solon: Is it? What makes an iPod valuable?

Tyro: Well, it just is. Everyone wants one.

Solon: I do not want an iPod.

Tyro: Well, if you had one, you could sell it and buy something else. That proves that an iPod is valuable.

Solon: What if no one wanted to buy my hypothetical iPod?

Tyro: Someone would want to buy it.

Solon: Why?

Tyro: Because an iPod is valuable.

Solon: You seem to be going in circles, my friend. You just argued that an iPod is valuable because it is valuable. That, by the way, is called "begging the question."

Tyro: Okay. I see what you mean. But do you really not want an iPod, Solon?

Solon: I can think of many other things I would rather possess or do. This beautiful day, for instance, brings me more happiness than an iPod ever could. After all, here I am sharing your company.

Tyro: So, this beautiful, rainy day is valuable?

Solon: No, the day itself has no value, just like an iPod is not itself valuable. What can be said correctly is that "I" value this day. No thing is valuable in and of itself. Not days, not iPods, certainly not money.

Tyro: Food has value in and of itself. Without food, we would die. We value food because we need food.

Solon: You may properly say that you value food because it helps you stay alive. You may even say that you "need" food *to stay alive*. But even those ideas do not mean food is intrinsically valuable. What if you did not want to stay alive?

Tyro: That's crazy. Everyone wants to stay alive.

Solon: Do they? Even though most people want to stay alive at most times, sometimes people no longer value even life itself, in which case, they do not need food. I have known people who wanted to die.

Tyro: That's an unhappy thought, for sure.

Solon: Yes, perhaps. But for some people in particular circumstances, life itself no longer makes them happy. For such people, food has no value. Even food cannot be an absolute need. Need is a contingent concept, contingent entirely on what a person values.

Tyro: (after a silence) I guess I see what you mean. If food is not itself valuable in and of itself, it's hard to think of anything that is.

Solon: That is because no "thing" has value in and of itself. People confer value on things. Value is utterly subjective, depending entirely on each particular human's mind.

Tyro: Well, people usually think food is valuable, don't they?

Solon: Certainly, Tyro. Still, all people do not value food the same. Some people place much greater value on food than other people.

Tyro: I see what you mean. That's what you mean when you define value as "psychic satisfaction that occurs in an individual human mind," right?

Solon: Just so, Tyro. No mind, no value. Value always occurs in a unique, individual mind.

Tyro: Why do we value some things and not others?

Solon: I think you already know. Why did you want to play golf today?

Tyro: I get it. We value what makes us happy.

WHAT WE VALUE

> *A system of morality which is based on relative emotional values is a mere illusion, a thoroughly vulgar conception which has nothing sound in it and nothing true.*
>
> SOCRATES[47]

What is moral and what is virtuous both depend on what humans value. Morality is founded rationally, not sentimentally, on all souls valuing all other souls as ontological equals. Virtue is founded on values that allow humans to achieve *eudaimonia*. Consequently, understanding what value is and what humans value is fundamental to understanding morality and virtue.

Eudaimonia is a psychological state of mind. How different people achieve *eudaimonia* depends entirely on what different people value. Individuals achieve *eudaimonia* in part by what economists call "consumption" of goods and services that particular individuals happen to value.

Strange as it may seem, the word "consumption" is a technical term in economics that includes an enormous variety of human actions; for example, engaging in activities (such as playing golf, eating food, listening to Mozart, going to the theatre, reading a poem, helping others, etc.); using objects (such as cars, computers, televisions, stereos, clothes, houses, etc.); possessing objects (such as paintings of Monet, jewelry, gold, land, antique furniture, etc.); experiencing reality (such as hearing crickets chirp in a glade, watching fireflies in a meadow at night, looking down from the rim of the Grand Canyon, walking across the Golden Gate, etc.).

For Tyro, playing golf is a means of achieving the ultimate end he desires. But some other person might find playing golf more like serious pain. Several aphorisms express the idea of the absolute individuality and subjectivity of value. "One man's trash is another man's treasure." "Beauty is in the eye of the beholder." "One man's meat is another man's poison." "One man gathers what another man spills." "There's no accounting for taste."

Value always resides in a unique, individual, private human mind. Value is not an intrinsic property of material objects, human activities, or even human qualities. No "thing" has intrinsic value in and of itself, even though we commonly speak as if things do have value. As Solon says, "no mind, no value."

Most people value a broad range of qualities in themselves and in others; for example: affection, altruism, artistry, beauty, bravery, brilliance, caring, charm, compassion, dependability, discipline, devotion, empathy, enthusiasm, expertise, fidelity, friendliness, freedom, generosity, grace, gallantry, honesty, humility, humor, industry, ingenuity, integrity, kindness, love, loyalty, modesty, optimism, patience, persistence, pleasantness, resilience, saintliness, self-control, serenity, thrift, trustworthiness, understanding, valor, wisdom, and zeal. But like objects and activities, none of these human qualities has intrinsic value in and of itself. Indeed, different persons place different value, if any at all, on each of the qualities listed above. We humans confer value on such qualities when we find them present in ourselves or others, just as we confer value on material objects. We value such human qualities, if we do, because they make us happy when we find them in ourselves or others.

Even though each human mind is independently the sole source of value, and even though each human mind confers value uniquely, nearly all people seem to hold several core values. Most people value life itself, self determination, freedom, true friendship, and the happiness of other people we care about. Yet, even though most people share these core values, we don't all agree on their relative importance. Some individuals value staying alive so highly that they are willing to give up some amount of self determination and freedom in return for the possibility of greater personal safety. Some individuals value true friendship so highly that they are willing to sacrifice their own lives to preserve the life of a true friend. Some individuals value self determination and freedom so highly that they would rather perish than be enslaved. As it happens, the core values that most people hold are frequently conflicting, requiring the sacrifice of some of one for more of another.

Value is psychic satisfaction that occurs in an individual mind. Notice that value occurs in "a" human mind. Value is not and cannot be a social or collective phenomenon, notwithstanding all the language we hear that claims it is. Put as simply and directly as it can be put, the concept of "social value" is vacuous. For no social mind exists in which social value could occur. I have a mind, which is a fact that I alone can know without doubt. I believe you have a mind, but I cannot experience your mind. "We" do not have a mind; we each have separate, unique, private, individual minds. Why dilate on such an obvious point? Because the mistaken, misleading notion of "social value" is so pervasive in our language.

Perhaps people who use the term "social value" do so in an attempt to make what they themselves value sound important, imperative, and universal. Politicians of all stripes engage in utter nonsense and meaningless jabber when they use expressions like "the common good," "our national interest," "the good of the nation," "Americans believe," "our human needs," and countless other phrases based on collective nouns. Collectives don't value anything. Only the individuals who comprise a collective can value, and they do so individually, not socially.

The use of collective nouns in political argument is a powerful rhetorical trope, to be sure. Using collective nouns as if they were individuals makes it sound like we all value the same things and to the same degree. We do not. "We" do not value anything. "I" value many things. "You" value many things. You and I may both value the same things, and even to something like the same degree—sometimes. Still, "we" cannot value anything. That idea is worth repeating; value is everywhere and always an individual phenomenon that occurs in an individual mind.

The only sense in which the idea of social value could be meaningful is if all persons in a society agreed unanimously about the value of something, and agreed unanimously to the same degree. And even in that highly unlikely case, we each have an individual, unique, private valuation, not a social valuation. We are hard pressed to identify any object, action, or human quality that even just two persons both value exactly the same, never mind *all* the individuals who comprise a society.

Yet, it is fair to say that individuals sometimes value objects, actions, or human qualities "in a social context." Voting is an example of people valuing and choosing something in a social context. But unless the outcome of voting is unanimous, the outcome can hardly be called a "social choice," even though it can be called a choice reached in a "social context." Some readers may think the distinction between "social choice" and "choosing in a social context" is little more than a trivial distinction. Hardly; chapters that follow explain why the distinction is vitally important, if we want to flourish together in a society. Political institutions and conventions, such as voting and majority rule, do not determine or reveal social value. The term "social value" is a great deceiver.

What we want and what we value matter because they are the basis of how we choose, which is the topic of the next section. How we choose matters because moral conduct is chosen conduct.

HOW WE CHOOSE

> *... every action and choice, is thought to aim at some good; and for this reason the good has rightly been declared to be that at which all things aim.*
>
> ARISTOTLE[48]

Solon: Can you think of nothing you would rather do today than play golf, Tyro?

Tyro: Today is Saturday; I am not in school; I have already finished my homework. No, I can't think of a single thing that would make me happier than playing golf today, if it doesn't rain.

Solon: You could play golf in the rain, if you choose.

Tyro: Playing golf in the rain is not much fun. Anyway, if it rains too much, the golf course will not be open. I would have no choice, in that case.

Solon: What if it does rain hard today? What will you choose then?

Tyro: I might like to go to a movie, but not as much as I would like playing golf. But if it rains, we could go to a movie. Would you like to go?

Solon: Maybe. So, if you can choose between playing golf and going to a movie, you will choose to play golf because you place greater value on golfing today than you place on watching a movie?

Tyro: Yes, definitely. If it's not raining later today, I choose golf.

Solon: Some people will choose to go see a movie today even if it does not rain. Why, do you suppose that is?

Tyro: Probably because some people don't like playing golf.

Solon: I like playing golf, but I also like watching good movies. If it does not rain today, I might still prefer going to see a movie.

Tyro: If you do choose a movie, that would mean you value going to a movie more than you value playing golf today, right?

Solon: Just so, Tyro. I, like every other human at all times, choose actions I believe will give me the greatest value. I do so because achieving the greatest value brings me my greatest happiness. I believe you said one of your teachers called that the "Fundamental Hypothesis of Economics."

―⁂―

People choose. When choice is possible and imminent, which requires at a minimum two or more feasible and mutually exclusive actions, people choose by comparing their alternatives and deciding which alternative they believe will yield them the greatest value, the greatest contribution toward achieving *eudaimonia*. Which is to say, people choose in accord with the Fundamental Hypothesis of Economics.

The FHE is a statement about human nature. Experience and reason suggest strongly that the FHE is a true statement about human nature. Of course, readers must make their own evaluations of the FHE. Whether the FHE is true or not has important implications for understanding human nature, and therefore for understanding what is moral and understanding why some people sometimes behave immorally.

―⁂―

Tyro: The FHE seems to say that people are selfish. Do you think that people are by their very nature selfish?

Solon: What do you mean by "selfish," Tyro?

Tyro: Everyone knows what "selfish" means.

Solon: Since everyone knows, then you know, too. Tell me what "selfish" means.

Tyro: Selfish means caring about what you yourself want and not caring about what anyone else wants.

Solon: Do you care about what anyone else wants?
Tyro: Of course; I'm not selfish.
Solon: Why do you care what someone else wants?
Tyro: Because I don't want to be selfish.
Solon: Why do you not want to be selfish?
Tyro: Because we should care about other people.
Solon: Why?
Tyro: (after some thought) If I didn't care about other people I would be selfish, and that's bad.
Solon: Why is it bad not to care about what other people want?
Tyro: Because that would be selfish.
Solon: Tyro, you seem to be going around in a circle again. You said that being selfish is not caring about what other people want. Then you said we should care about what other people want, because not caring is bad, and that it is bad because not caring for other people is selfish. Do you see that you are begging the question about why selfishness is bad?
Tyro: (looking less than happy) Yes. But I have always been taught that not caring about what other people want is selfish, and that being selfish is bad.
Solon: You no doubt have been taught that being selfish is bad; but why would it be bad to want your own happiness?
Tyro: It cannot be bad to want happiness for ourselves. But we should also want happiness for others, shouldn't we?
Solon: We each want to be happy by our very nature. But why do we care about the happiness of others?
Tyro: I care about the happiness of others because it makes me feel bad if I don't and it makes me feel good when I do.
Solon: Does that not mean that you care about the happiness of other people because it brings happiness to you?
Tyro: Yes.
Solon: Is that not selfish?
Tyro: I think you are trying to trick me.

Solon: No, Tyro. I am trying to see if you can give meaning to the word "selfish" that does not make every choice anyone ever makes a selfish choice.

Tyro: If the FHE is correct—if we all always choose those actions that yield the greatest value to us—then it would seem that we always choose selfishly.

Solon: Just so, Tyro. But "selfish" is not a word that I would use. I think the FHE is correct. The FHE is a statement about human nature that I am persuaded is true. What do you think?

Tyro: The FHE seems to be true about most of my own choices, but sometimes I am altruistic, too.

Solon: What does it mean to be "altruistic"?

Tyro: Altruism means caring about the welfare and happiness of others over and above caring about one's own welfare and happiness.

Solon: Why should people care about the welfare and happiness of others over and above one's own? Please do not say "because it is good to care about the welfare and happiness of others."

Tyro: Yes, yes, I know; that would beg the question. I can see that I'm running into the same problem with altruism that I ran into with selfishness. The statements "selfishness is bad," and "altruism is good" are both opinions. They are both statements about what someone values or what someone should value.

Solon: Excellent, Tyro! Now, let us cut to the chase, as they say. Why does anyone value anything, whether the thing is an object, an action, or even a human quality?

Tyro: Because the thing generates happiness in the mind of the person doing the valuing.

Solon: You never cease to amaze me, Tyro! You are correct. Now what of selfishness and altruism?

Tyro: If I give a homeless man money, I do so because it makes *me* happy. So, I suppose someone could say that I am altruistic because I am selfish. How odd, though, to call altruistic behavior selfish.

Solon: I prefer not to call people or their behaviors selfish or altruistic, Tyro. I cannot give meaning to either term that distinguishes the behavior of one human from another. I think the Fundamental Hypothesis of Economics is correct. I think that all people choose those actions that they believe will bring them the greatest happiness. That seems to me to be the nature of humans.

Tyro: So, people are selfish by nature? Somehow that seems so tawdry and base. Is that really human nature?

Solon: Tyro, you seem to be trapped by your words. Why do you say interest in one's own happiness is tawdry and base? Suppose people were not self interested. Suppose people did not care about their own happiness. Can you even imagine such a world? Let us try. Let us visit Threesville, as it would be if people were interested only in the wellbeing and happiness of others above their own wellbeing and happiness.

Annie: Hi Bobby. Lovely day today. I'm here to do whatever will make you happy.

Bobby: Yes, it is a fine day, but no, no; the question is what can I do for you?

Annie: Wouldn't you like me to hoe your corn?

Bobby: No, I will hoe the corn. The corn is not mine, of course. The corn is for you and Callie, not for me. I will take only as much corn as needed to keep me alive.

Annie: I would never be so selfish, Bobby. You and Callie shall have most of the corn, not me. I'll take only a small amount to stay alive.

Bobby: (a little frustrated) Perhaps Callie will want most of the corn. In any case, I will hoe the corn.

Annie: I can't let you do that Bobby. The reason I'm here is to help others.

Callie: Hi Annie; hi Bobby. I'm a bit hungry and would like to buy some of your corn Bobby. What is the price. I have eggs today. I would like a bushel of corn. How many eggs will you require?

Bobby: I will trade you a bushel of corn for one dozen eggs; no wait! Let's say only eight eggs.

Callie: That's ridiculous, Bobby. Your price is way too low; you must accept at least two dozen eggs for a bushel of corn.

Bobby: You insult me, Callie. On second thought, I will trade a bushel of corn to you for just six eggs.

Callie: (in a bit of a huff) Fine! I don't think it's right, but here are your six eggs. Incidentally, I'm taking no more than half a bushel of corn for them. That will mean I can't make as much corn bread, of course, but I don't mind. I'm here to serve others. I will make do with half the corn bread I had in mind.

Tyro: That's just silly.

Solon: You are right, Tyro. The very idea of people not being interested in their own happiness is unimaginably silly.

Tyro: (after a longish silence) If we always make choices that bring us the greatest happiness, why do so many people say that self interest is bad and that placing the welfare of others above one's own welfare is good?

Solon: I suppose that some people say it just because it is what they were taught. Perhaps we are taught that selfishness is bad and altruism is good because if we believe it, that belief gives some people power over us to get what they themselves value. That motive has certainly been a factor throughout the history of nation-states and religious organizations.

Tyro: What do you mean?

Solon: Think Threesville, Tyro. If Annie tells Callie that she is behaving selfishly, Annie evidently wants Callie to behave differently. The

Human Nature

[handwritten note: What if everyone was selfish & just made themselves happy & everyone happy?]

different behavior that Annie wants will bring Annie happiness at Callie's expense.

Tyro: So, humans by nature are selfish? We should just get used to it?

Solon: You are persistent in clinging to that word, Tyro. As I said, I do not use the word "selfish." You can use the word if you like, but it seems that all you will really be saying if you do use the word is that humans are human.

Choice requires at least contemplation of action, if not action itself. When people contemplate any particular action, taking no action always becomes at once an alternative, thereby constituting the necessary second feasible alternative required for any choice whatsoever. More frequently, though, taking no action whatsoever is a third alternative among two or more feasible alternatives that require overt action. For example, I may contemplate eating an egg, eating a banana, or eating nothing at all. Consequently, once I have entertained the possibility of feasible action, I will choose, even if I take no overt action.

Most people, whether they are particularly religious people or not, believe, as did René Descartes[49] and Thomas Reid,[50] that humans are something more than matter and energy. Some prefer to call that part of humans that is not matter and energy "mind," while others prefer to call it "soul." The notion that humans comprise both body and soul (or mind, if you prefer) is perhaps the most famous of all philosophical dualisms. Most people are persuaded that they do indeed have the power to choose (a.k.a., free will), regardless of whether they attribute that power to mind or to soul.

Humans have a nature, notwithstanding the ideas of Jean-Paul Sartre, who argued that we humans are free to choose our own essence, and are therefore "condemned to be free."[51] Sartre is correct about choice; we are free to choose, but we choose for an overarching reason—to achieve *eudaimonia*. We are not automatons, nor do we behave randomly; we humans choose our behavior, even though we choose for reasons. And of course, willful choice, or at least believing ourselves to be capable of willful choice, is a necessary condition for our ability to behave morally.

Understanding how people choose helps us understand why people sometimes behave immorally. Immoral behavior is a choice. If the FHE is correct, then people who behave immorally must believe that their immoral behavior will bring them greater value (and therefore happiness) than behaving morally would. Plato thought that if people knew what is good for them, they would do it. Perhaps Plato was right. Perhaps people who behave immorally do so due to ignorance. Perhaps they simply do not know that in the end, immoral behavior will not contribute to their happiness.

3

How We Know What Is Moral

The only source of knowledge is experience.

ALBERT EINSTEIN[52]

There is nothing in the intellect that was not first in the senses ... except the intellect itself.

GOTTFRIED WILHELM LEIBNIZ[53]

True knowledge exists in knowing that you know nothing.

SOCRATES

We are here and it is now. Further than that all human knowledge is moonshine.

H. L. MENCKEN[54]

HOW WE KNOW ANYTHING

Our rationality, which is fundamentally part of our human nature, and our ability to know, are necessary conditions for us to be bound by the moral law. But how do we know the moral law? We come to know the moral law the same way we come to know anything at all.

Of course, people most often learn what they take themselves to know from testimony of others. Someone taught us. We learn arithmetic from our grade school teachers; we learn about religion from our parents, priests, pastors, and ministers; we learn about the world by reading the testimony of others. Thank goodness, for if we each had to learn what we know from our own experiences alone, or by our own ability to reason alone, we could not know much, given the shortness of our lives.

Knowledge is a true, justified belief, according to Plato and countless others who have thought about the word.[55] But how does someone come to have a true, justified belief *originally*, before anyone else knew it and latter taught it? Humans come to know *originally* in just two ways—by experience or by reasoning. Experience requires our sensory capacities. Reasoning requires thinking. Ability to sense and ability to reason are both essential parts of our human nature that allow us to know.

Some philosophers, called "empiricists," argue that all human knowledge comes from experience. Surprisingly, Einstein seems to have been an empiricist, based on his statements, notwithstanding his enormous capacity for thinking. "Nothing is in the mind that was not first in the senses" is a well-known expression of that idea. The British empiricists, Thomas Hobbes, David Hume, and John Locke, who lived and wrote in the 17th to 18th centuries, are among the most well known philosophers who thought that our senses are the means of all that we come to know. But the idea of empiricism dates to antiquity; Aristotle may have been the first empiricist of note in written history.

Other philosophers called "rationalists" think that at least some human knowledge can come from thinking alone. René Descartes, Baruch Spinoza, Gottfried Leibniz, and Immanuel Kant, who also lived and wrote in the 17th to 18th centuries, were rationalists. But, of course, the idea of humans knowing by means other than experience is also ancient. Plato, Aristotle's teacher, thought that humans possess a kind of innate

How We Know What Is Moral

[handwritten: HOW?]

knowledge that isn't acquired through experience, but which can be awakened by thinking.

Plato's dialogue, *Meno*, proposes that mathematics is an example of such innate knowledge. The Pythagorean Theorem, often expressed in symbols as $a^2+b^2=c^2$, states a property of right triangles that would not likely ever be discovered experientially by measuring a bunch of triangles that appear to have one 90-degree angle. Yet, in the *Meno*, Socrates leads a young slave boy, who had no previous training in mathematics, to discovering and understanding the Pythagorean Theorem for himself, by reason alone. [handwritten: doesn't reason come from experience?]

Experience and reason are not really two independent or mutually exclusive ways of knowing. They are complementary. What we come to know by experience often makes sense in terms of reasoning, and what makes sense to us by reasoning can often be demonstrated in experience. Arithmetic is a good example. We can know that 2+2=4 is a true statement by reason alone, but we also know by the experience of counting.

Experience and reason are usually found together to justify what people take themselves to know. The facts do not speak for themselves. What we observe with our senses requires mediation by our thinking to result in knowledge. The sun is not about the size of a big beach ball, nor does it travel in a circle around the earth, regardless of what it looks like. Could anyone figure out the rules of baseball just by observing lots of baseball games? Sensory input alone does not produce knowledge. But what could a rational, thinking person come to know, if that person possessed none of our usual five primary senses? Thinking alone, with no sensory input, may also fall short of knowing.

Tyro: Solon, you asked me the other day how I know that stealing is wrong. Maybe I don't know. Maybe it's just my opinion that stealing is wrong. How do we know anything at all? Maybe we don't really know anything for sure.

Solon: That is what some philosophers called "skeptics" think. But I do not think so. I agree with René Descartes, who wrote in French, *Je pense donc je suis*, more commonly known in Latin as the "*cogito*"—*cogito, ergo sum*, I think, therefore I am.[56]

Tyro: So, Descartes thought that because he was thinking he could know that he existed?

Solon: No. Descartes thought that because he was thinking he had irrefutable evidence that he was a thinking thing. Existence? That is a conversation for later.

Tyro: So, Descartes thought that since there he was, thinking, and aware that he was thinking, he definitely could know that he was a thinking thing. He could know at least that much without doubt.

Solon: Just so, Tyro! To be deceived about being a thinking thing, or to doubt that one is a thinking thing, one has to be a thinking thing. Doubt is thinking.

Tyro: Okay, I see how we can know we are thinking things. So, we can at least know something for sure. So, how *do* we know that stealing is wrong? And what does it mean to say we know something in the first place?

Solon: Let us start with the easier question first. We can identify three necessary conditions for knowing. If you know something, that means you have a true, justified belief.

Tyro: I definitely believe stealing is wrong.

Solon: You no doubt do believe that stealing is wrong. But why do you believe? Is a statement true just because you believe it?

Tyro: No; I see your point. It's the other way around. We are entitled to believe something *if* it's true, but something is not true just because we believe it.

Solon: Correct, Tyro! Why do you believe the statement "stealing is wrong" is true? Are you justified in that belief? And an even more challenging question—*is* the statement true? Do you meet the necessary conditions for saying you know that stealing is wrong?

Tyro: I'm beginning to think that I cannot say that I know that stealing is wrong; I can say only that I believe it is. What does it mean to be justified in a belief?

Solon: Justification means that we have reasonable, persuasive evidence that some statement is true. By the way, statements are the only "somethings" that can be true or false.

Tyro: The statement "stealing is wrong" doesn't seem to be a truth claim about reality. It seems to be a statement about my opinion of stealing.

Solon: Humans are part of reality. If there is such a thing as "right" human conduct, that conduct would also be part of reality, would it not?

Tyro: Yes. Is there such a thing as "right" human conduct?

Solon: We have already had that conversation, Tyro. What do you say in answer to your own question?

Tyro: The Moral Imperative—do not compel unjustly—implies logically that compelling another is wrong human conduct, and by logic, implies that right human conduct is all behavior that does not compel.

Solon: Your memory and understanding of our earlier conversation is accurate, Tyro. The statement "stealing is wrong" is a truth claim about reality, for the statement "not stealing is right human conduct" is a truth claim about reality, if right human conduct exists.

Tyro: Exists? You said we would talk about existence later. I guess later is now. What do you mean by "exists"?

Solon: What do you think it means to "exist," Tyro?

Tyro: (wanting to say "I asked you first," but not saying it) Something exists if it's here.

Solon: What do you mean by "it's here"?

Tyro: I mean we can see it. No, wait! If something exists we can see it, hear it, taste it, smell it, or touch it. We can experience what exists with our senses.

Solon: Yes, but can you see, hear, taste, smell, or touch ultraviolet radiation?

Tyro: How did I know something like that question was coming? No, I can't see ultraviolet radiation.

Solon: But you believe that ultraviolet radiation exists, do you not?

Tyro: Yes. Scientists say so.

Solon: Do you believe whatever scientists say? Scientists used to say that the sun revolves around the earth and that radio waves travel through an ether.

Tyro: (a little exasperated) Okay, so what do *you* mean by exists?

Solon: "Existence" means the same thing that a statement being true means. If a statement is true, it is so because the statement corresponds with reality. As W.V.O. Quine said, "no sentence is true but reality makes it so."[57] Conversely, if a statement is false, it is false because the statement does not correspond with reality.

Tyro: You still haven't told me what you mean when you use the word "exists."

Solon: Fair enough. The only meaning I have for the word "exists" is that humans can somehow perceive that which we say exists.

Tyro: Your meaning for "exists" sounds like what I said. Something exists if we can perceive it with one or more of our senses.

Solon: Yes, or if we can invent some device that allows us to perceive it. We can perceive ultraviolet radiation with photodiodes and photocathodes, but we cannot perceive them directly with any of our natural senses. Yet, we are told by scientists that bees can perceive ultraviolet radiation directly, by their bee nature.

Tyro: (with a gleeful smile) Do you believe whatever scientists say?

Solon: I have no reason to doubt them when it comes to bees; I am persuaded they are correct about bees. Of course, I have some reservations about certain other truth claims that some scientists have made.

Tyro: Would you say you *know* that bees can perceive ultraviolet radiation directly?

Solon: I would say I have a justified belief, but I would also say that I do not know that bees perceive ultraviolet radiation. We humans know much less than we usually take ourselves to know.

Tyro: So, if something exists, humans can somehow perceive it?

Solon: No. If humans can somehow perceive it, humans might have justification for believing that something exists.

Tyro: That observation implies that some things could exist that humans might not know anything about.

Solon: Just so, my perceptive friend. Something being the case, and humans knowing it is the case, are not at all the same thing. Philosophical skeptics do not think there is no reality to know about; they think we are not justified in believing what we take ourselves to know about reality.

Tyro: So, based on experiential evidence we get from our senses, or from some device we invent that augments our senses, we come to believe that some statements are true or false?

Solon: Just so, Tyro. I do not think we can know that truth claims about matter and energy are true or false, but we can be and often are persuaded one way or the other by empirical evidence from our senses.

Tyro: One of my science teachers told us that we can sometimes prove that a hypothesis is false. She called it "falsifying" a hypothesis based on experimental evidence that proves the hypothesis is false.

Solon: Proof is a very high bar, Tyro. Some philosophers agree that falsification of some statements may be possible, if the statements are false. Karl Popper thought so. But I don't think that falsification is necessarily possible, even for statements that are false.

Tyro: Why not?

Solon: Suppose someone makes the statement "there are no black swans." Suppose that after years and years of searching for black swans, none are found. Would the evidence of not finding any black swans prove the statement to be true?

Tyro: Not finding any black swans after many years would be rather persuasive evidence, but I can see that no amount of confirming evidence would *prove* with certainty that the statement is true.

Solon: Excellent, Tyro! Now, suppose that just about everyone came to believe that black swans do not exist. Then, one day, someone finds a black swan. Would that new evidence falsify the statement "there are no black swans"?

Tyro: I think so. Certainly.

Solon: But what if someone said, after seeing the black creature, "that is not a swan; it cannot be a swan, since it is black."

Tyro: (with a most perplexed expression on his face) I'll have to think about that example for a while.

Solon: Please do. Let us try an easier question. Can we know the statement "the sky is blue today" is true?

Tyro: Hmmm. Maybe I can't really know the sky is blue today, but can't I be justified in believing that it is?

Solon: Definitely, Tyro. We are persuaded by sensory evidence that the sky is blue today.

Tyro: Our senses can sometimes deceive us, and some humans don't even have all five senses. That possibility seems to suggest that we might not ever be able to say for sure that we know a particular statement is true or false.

Solon: Excellent, Tyro! Most of what we take ourselves to know is only "probably" true. At best, we are persuaded by our senses—our experiences—that one or another statement is true or false. Science, that branch of philosophy that uses the scientific method, searches for true statements just that way.

Tyro: But science and the scientific method seem unusually reliable. In fact, my science teacher at school tells us many things about the universe, which he represents as being absolutely true. We are

Tyro: required to remember such truths for exams in school. Should we doubt what scientists tell us?

Solon: The best scientists are always skeptical about what they think they know. They understand that what they take themselves to know today is contingent on the next round of observation, experimentation, and thinking about the evidence tomorrow.

Tyro: But scientists usually speak as if they are certain about what they know.

Solon: We all have to believe we know many things, just to get by in life from day to day. When your science teachers are trying to teach something about the universe, they are not trying, just then, to teach you what it means to "know" and what it means for a statement to be "true." We can overlook that they speak as if they are certain. The best scientists know that what they take to be fact is really just a statement about matter, energy, and time, which they are persuaded is true, given the evidence so far.

Tyro: So, even what most people call a "fact" isn't necessarily true?

Solon: You are such a good student, Tyro! Just so! A "fact" is usually just a statement that lots of people are persuaded is true. Sometimes it is really helpful to ask ourselves what it is that persuades us that some particular fact is true. If we did, we probably would not call so many statements "facts."

Tyro: The statement "the sky is blue today" seems to be a different kind of statement than "stealing is wrong." Somehow, the statement "stealing is wrong" seems like it could be just an opinion.

Solon: You are on the right track, Tyro. The two statements are different in a fundamental way. Can you tell me how they are different?

Tyro: We are justified in believing that the statement "the sky is blue today" is true because we can see it with our own eyes. Our evidence is experiential. We just use our sense of sight, which persuades us that the sky really is blue today. But we cannot use one of our five senses to justify belief in the truth of the statement "stealing is wrong."

Solon: Excellent, Tyro!
Tyro: What if I said "the blue sky is beautiful today." Wouldn't that statement be an opinion?
Solon: Yes, definitely. You would be giving a report about yourself and what you value, not so much about the sky, when you use the word "beautiful."
Tyro: Why isn't the statement "stealing is wrong" also just an opinion? If that statement isn't an opinion, you seem to be implying that we have at least three kinds of statements: statements like "the sky is blue today," statements like "the blue sky is beautiful today," and statements like "stealing is wrong."
Solon: Tyro, your powers of perception are truly impressive! You have identified three distinct kinds of statements. The first kind are statements we can be justified in believing based on evidence from our senses and experience. The second kind are statements that are opinions—statements about what someone values. Opinions are personal statements about the good, the bad, and the ugly, so to speak. Such statements cannot be true or false, for they are not truth claims about reality. Now for the missing piece. What is distinctive about the third kind of statement—statements like "stealing is wrong"?
Tyro: I'm drawing a blank. I still think the statement "stealing is wrong" seems like an opinion.
Solon: Yet, it is not. The statement "stealing is bad" would be an opinion. The word "bad" is a value assessment. The word "wrong" is not about someone's values. In the statement "stealing is wrong," "wrong" means "not right behavior for humans." Right and wrong do not mean the same things as good and bad.
Tyro: I'm still drawing a blank.
Solon: I will give you a hint. The statement "stealing is wrong" and the statement "2+2=4" have a fundamental quality in common.
Tyro: Yikes! Mathematics is not my strongest subject in school. How are those two statements similar?

Solon: Would you say that you know 2+2=4 is a true statement?
Tyro: Definitely. "2+2=4" is a statement that is necessarily true. It cannot be false.
Solon: Indeed, Tyro. If you know 2+2=4 is a true statement, then you must have a true, justified belief. What justifies your belief?
Tyro: I am justified in believing that 2+2=4 is a true statement by logic. My evidence is reasoning alone. I don't need sensory evidence to know that 2+2=4 is true.
Solon: Correct, Tyro! You have articulated the essential feature of our third kind of statement. We are justified in believing that 2+2=4 is a true statement by thinking alone. And so it is with the statement "stealing is wrong."
Tyro: How can I know that stealing is wrong by thinking alone?
Solon: By the Principle of Reciprocity and the laws of logic.

We make statements about what we take ourselves to know. These statements are one of three kinds. First, we have truth claims about reality that are true or false because reality makes them so. Statements of this type are sometimes called "synthetic, *a posteriori*" statements.[58] The Latin term "*a posteriori*" conveys the meaning "after experience," although that meaning is not a literal translation. Statements of this type may also be called "positive" statements," based on the meaning "to posit." We come to be persuaded that we know the truth or falsity of positive statements by repeated experience garnered from our senses, but mediated by our thinking. Thinking alone provides no evidence for knowing, when it comes to synthetic, *a posteriori* statements (a.k.a., positive statements).

Second, we have truth claims about reality that are necessarily true or false by logic and reasoning alone. We are definitely justified in believing that such statements are true or false by thinking alone. In fact, empirical evidence from our senses cannot justify our belief in such statements. Statements of this type are sometimes called "analytic, *a priori*" statements.[59] The Latin term "*a priori*" conveys the meaning "before experience." Statements of this type may also be called positive statements, which gives us two categories of positive statements—analytic and synthetic.

Third, we have statements of opinion, which are not truth claims about reality. Statements of this type are called "normative" statements. Normative statements are neither true nor false, for they are not truth claims about reality. Normative statements are really just expressions of what someone values, and nothing more. At the risk of being tedious, Exhibit 1 offers a few examples of the three types of statements. Exhibit 2 summarizes the taxonomy of statements.

Recognizing these three very different kinds of statements is important for reasonable discourse about moral philosophy and the political economy. Much of what people disagree about concerning the political economy is due to confusion or ambiguity about the kinds of statements we make. Most of the statements people disagree about when it comes to the political economy are normative statements.

Reasonable people can and do disagree about normative statements for one of three reasons. First, people may be ignorant of certain true positive statements. Second, people may have different values. Third, people who have similar values, and who are aware of relevant true positive statements, may weight the same values differently. Reaching agreement in a social context is more likely if we understand why we disagree.

How do we come to know the moral law? Of course, we first learn that stealing is wrong from testimony of others—our parents, usually. But with time, as children mature, they begin to understand for themselves that stealing is wrong. No one has to tell them; they know from personal, empirical evidence (how they feel about stealing). And with more time and maturity, they come to know by reason alone.

Exhibit 1. A Taxonomy of Statements

Statement	Type of Statement	Justification
That rock is a diamond	Positive, synthetic, *a posteriori*	Sensory perceptions, mediated by thinking
That rock is beautiful	Normative	Personal values
That rock is slate	Positive, synthetic, *a posteriori*	Sensory perceptions, mediated by thinking
That rock is ugly	Normative	Personal values
An elephant is in the corner	Positive, synthetic, *a posteriori*	Sensory perceptions, mediated by thinking
That elephant in the corner is pink	Positive, synthetic, *a posteriori*	Sensory perceptions, mediated by thinking
Elephants exist	Positive, synthetic, *a posteriori*	Sensory perceptions, mediated by thinking
The God of Abraham Exists	Positive, synthetic, *a posteriori*	Sensory perceptions, mediated by thinking
Something Has Always Existed	Positive, analytic, *a priori* (and necessarily true)	Thinking, validated by experience
2+2=4	Positive, analytic, *a priori* (and necessarily true)	Thinking, validated by experience
2+2=5	Positive, analytic, *a priori* (and necessarily false)	Thinking, validated by experience
2+2=4 is a thrilling truth	Normative	Personal Values
2+2=4 is true in all possible worlds	Positive, analytic, *a priori* (and necessarily true)	Thinking, validated by experience
Annie is Annie	Positive, analytic, *a priori* (and necessarily true)	Thinking, validated by experience
Annie is not Annie	Positive, analytic, *a priori* (and necessarily false)	Thinking, validated by experience
Annie is bad	Normative	Personal values
Annie is moral	Positive, synthetic, *a posteriori*	Sensory perceptions, mediated by thinking
Stealing is wrong	Positive, analytic, *a priori* (and necessarily true)	Thinking, validated by experience
Bobby should help Annie	Normative	Personal values
Callie is a thief	Positive, synthetic, *a posteriori*	Sensory perceptions, mediated by thinking
People have a right to health care	Positive, analytic, *a priori* (and necessarily false)	Thinking, validated by experience
Bobby should pay for Annie's health care	Normative	Personal values
Wealthy people ought to pay higher taxes	Normative	Personal values
Wealthy people pay higher taxes	Positive, synthetic, *a posteriori*	Sensory Perceptions, Mediated by Thinking

EXHIBIT 2
Taxonomy of Statements

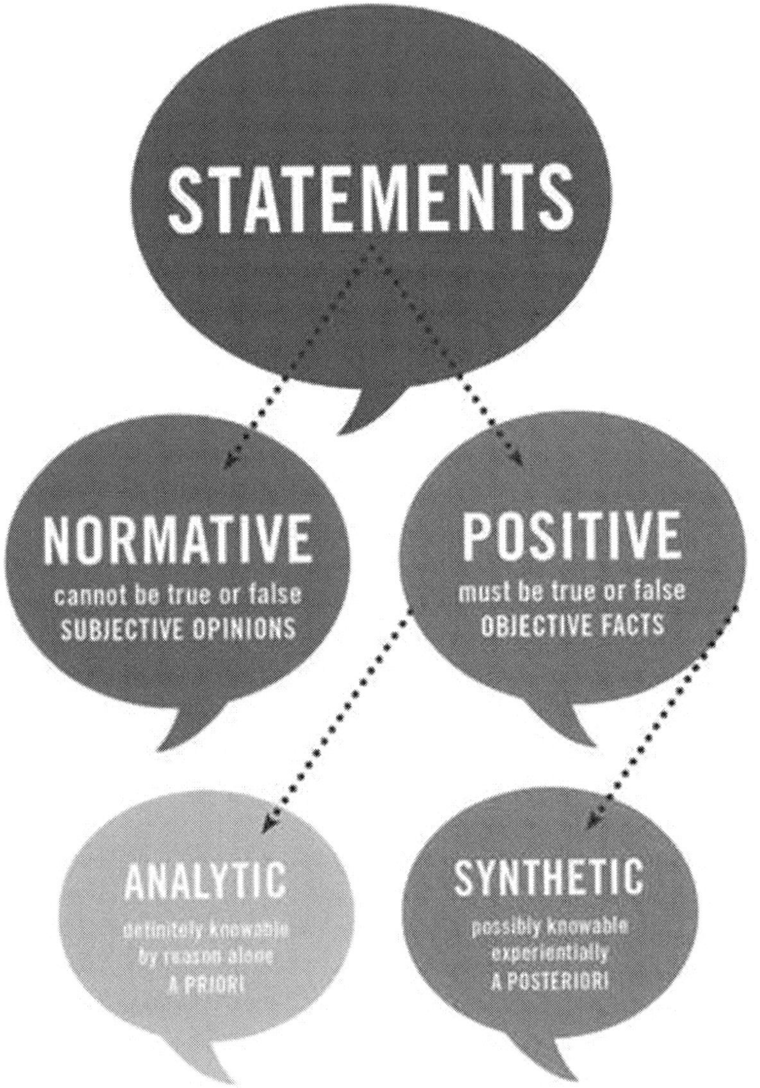

STATEMENTS

NORMATIVE
cannot be true or false
SUBJECTIVE OPINIONS

POSITIVE
must be true or false
OBJECTIVE FACTS

ANALYTIC
definitely knowable
by reason alone
A PRIORI

SYNTHETIC
possibly knowable
experientially
A POSTERIORI

JUSTIFICATION FROM EMOTION

If someone steals *your* possessions, *you* begin to know first hand that stealing is wrong. You know by how you feel about it. A theory called "emotivism," sometimes called "hurrah/boo" theory, holds that statements about right and wrong behavior are nothing more than normative expressions of how someone feels about some behavior.[60] Emotivism proposes that the statement "stealing is wrong" is equivalent to "boo, hiss on stealing." Stealing on this account isn't really wrong; it's just something someone doesn't like or feel good about.

Here is a different perspective. Emotions are part of our sensory apparatus; call them our sixth sense if you like. How we feel if someone steals from us is a sensation, not unlike sensations evoked by our other five primary senses. Like all sensations, emotions occur only in minds. Certain emotions are to human conduct as seeing is to light, hearing is to sound, smelling is to fragrance, tasting is to flavor, and touching is to material objects. Stealing evokes a sensory response in most humans that we call emotion, just as light evokes a sensory response in most people that we call seeing.

We humans can sense that stealing is wrong human conduct, just as surely as we sense the pain of touching a hot stove. If someone steals from us we may feel angry. We may feel unhappy. We may feel depressed. But we definitely feel. Even people who empathize with a thief, perhaps believing that stealing was justified by the thief's dire situation, may feel sadness that a fellow human resorted to stealing. Of course, most people blame a thief; empathizing with a thief is rather Zen-like. When someone steals *from us*, we begin to know at that instant that stealing is wrong, *for ourselves*—independently of the admonitions we may first have learned from our parents and teachers (by testimony).

Given sufficient maturity, most people also feel an emotional response if they steal another person's property. They feel guilt. Perhaps not immediately, perhaps not until they lie on their death bed. Granted, some people may never reach the level of maturity and rationality that enables feelings of guilt. Yet, it seems that most people do. But even people who feel no guilt *as thieves*, still feel anger, frustration, and unhappiness if someone steals from them. We all come to know that stealing is wrong human conduct, first by testimony of others and second by how we feel about it.

JUSTIFICATION FROM REASON

We do have another, more important way of knowing that stealing is wrong. The statement "stealing is wrong" is an analytic, *a priori* statement, because rational beings can and do know that stealing is wrong by thinking alone. The Principle of Reciprocity, introduced in Chapter 1, and logic, allow us to know by thinking alone that stealing is wrong human conduct.

The Principle of Reciprocity says that we can logically and reasonably expect to get from others what we give to them. Several aphorisms express the idea poetically. "What goes around comes around." "You reap what you sow." "What's good for the goose is good for the gander." Several verses from the Bible express the idea even more poetically. "Woe to the wicked! It shall be ill with him, for what his hands have dealt out shall be done to him" (Isaiah 3:11 ESV). "So whatever you wish that others would do to you, do also to them, for this is the Law and the Prophets" (Matthew 7:12, ESV). "Whoever digs a pit will fall into it, and a stone will come back on him who starts it rolling" (Proverbs 26:27, ESV).

As rational beings, we humans can and do understand the Principle of Reciprocity. The Principle of Reciprocity generates the Moral Imperative by logic alone.

Major Premise: Humans are rational, ontological equals (i.e., we are thinking beings and we all have the same rights as souls).
Minor Premise: Rational ontological equals know and agree with the Principle of Reciprocity (i.e., we expect to get behavior from others that we give them, and agree that we should).
Conclusion: Rational ontological equals agree that it is not right conduct to compel ontological equals unjustly.

In Threesville, Bobby knows he should not compel Annie or Callie, for if he does, he concedes to Annie and Callie the right to compel him. Doing so would be irrational. Bobby can and does know the Moral Imperative by reason alone, as do Annie and Callie, because they are rational and because they take themselves to be ontologically equal.

Try a strange, highly unrealistic, but highly instructive thought experiment. Suppose that in Threesville the universe were so constituted that by strange laws of nature, any compulsion of one by another was automatically and instantly reciprocated. If Bobby robbed Annie, Bobby would instantly be robbed himself, by natural law akin to gravity. If Callie murdered Bobby, Callie would instantly be murdered herself, by a law of nature. If Annie defrauded Bobby, Annie would instantly be defrauded herself. Any form of unjust compulsion whatsoever would be instantly reciprocated on the perpetrator of compulsion in this fanciful, imaginary world. How would the citizens of Threesville behave in such a world? Because they are rational, Annie, Bobby, and Callie would behave according to the Moral Imperative. They would not compel one another.

Like so many other truths that we take ourselves to know, we know the moral law by a confluence of reason and experience. Of the two, reason is more important, since synthetic *a posteriori* statements cannot be *proved* by confirmatory evidence. At best, the truth value of synthetic, *a posteriori* statements is a question of probability. We are able to judge the truth of synthetic, *a posteriori* statements to be more or less probable, but we cannot know for sure. But rational beings can know with certainty the truth value of analytic, *a priori* statements. The statement "stealing is wrong" is analytic, *a priori*. Socrates seems to have gotten it right. We humans know very little. Still, because we are rational beings, we can and do know the moral law with certainty.

—⁂—

Tyro: Don't some people believe that we can know in a third way—by divine revelation? Don't some people believe that we know stealing is wrong because God said so?

Solon: Many people do so believe. St. Thomas Aquinas certainly thought so. But even if the moral law is revealed divinely, we do not require divine revelation to know the Moral Imperative; such truth can be known by humans by reason alone.

Tyro: Do you think divine revelation is a way for humans to know about the universe?

Solon: I cannot rule out absolutely the possibility of divine revelation, but I also cannot claim that I know any particular claim of divine revelation is false or true.

Tyro: Can't scientists help us out here?

Solon: Scientists really have no more to say about divine revelation than anyone else. Some scientists do rule out divine revelation as a way of knowing, but some scientists do not. Scientists usually rely on evidence produced by application of the scientific method to justify what they think they know. The scientific method relies on sensory observation, mediated by thinking. What people call divine revelation is a particular category of testimony.

Tyro: Relying on claims of divine revelation as a source of knowledge seems to require some sort of faith.

Solon: That, my young friend, is an astute observation. I think you are right.

―∞―

St. Thomas Aquinas began the *Summa Theologica* with a defense of divine revelation.[61] In fact, Aquinas considered sacred doctrine to be a science that transcends all others. Yet, if someone claims to have had a personal divine revelation, it's not clear how anyone else could know whether that person is delusional, reporting a perceived state of reality, or perhaps just lying.

Most people have not experienced divine revelation personally. But if they did personally experience what they took to be a divine revelation, they would doubtlessly believe whatever had been revealed to them.

They would also likely want to tell others. In antiquity, several people did just that. Later on, other people used the testimony of those ancient writers to persuade, to instruct, to edify, to enrich, to command, and in many cases, as warrant *to compel* multitudes of other people unjustly.

Yet, in the end, claims of divine revelation are testimony. If we believe claims of divine revelation, it seems that we do so by faith. But what is faith? Mark Twain quipped that "faith is believing what you know ain't so."[62] That remark may seem a bit harsh, especially to people of faith, even though some people of faith smile at least a little when they read it. Is it possible that faith is believing some truth claim simply because we choose to? Are we not free to believe whatever we choose to believe?

The British philosopher Colin McGinn rejects the possibility of "choosing" to believe something (as do many other philosophers).[63] We believe or disbelieve positive statements about the cosmos for reasons. We don't just "choose" to believe anything. A simple example seems to make the case; can you will yourself to believe that Santa Clause is alive and well at the North Pole? No? It seems we come to believe what we believe because we are *persuaded* by a confluence of experience and reason. We take ourselves to be justified in what we believe; it seems that we don't believe anything just because we *decided* to believe. We are persuaded in a variety of ways: by testimony, by reason, by our senses, by our emotions, by our delusions, by respect for authority, by tradition—the list of what may persuade us is long. But we are persuaded to believe; we do not just choose our beliefs.

Perhaps for some people, belief in divine revelation comes down to trust. First, people of faith somehow come to believe in an omniscient, omnipotent, all good, and gracious God—let us call that description of God the "God of Abraham." Second, perhaps people of faith reason that God would not permit misrepresentation of his nature or his will for humans. Third, perhaps people of faith believe whoever claims to be reporting a divine revelation, because true believers *trust* that God would not permit a lie or an error in divine revelation. Perhaps people who profess to believe divine revelation as a matter of faith are really just

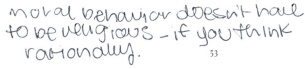

trusting in the God of Abraham, who they have somehow already come to believe exists. Such trust would seem to be rational, *if* one already believed in an all knowing, all powerful, all good, gracious God, the God of the world's best-known and most prevalent religions.

For agnostics and atheists, faith is not a rational basis for believing divine revelation. Consequently, people who do not already believe in the God of Abraham, usually do not accept divine revelation as a way of knowing. For such people, basing one's belief in the God of Abraham on divine revelation itself—such as writings in the Talmud, the Bible, or the Quran—seems to put the cart before the horse. It seems reasonable to believe divine revelation on faith, *if one already believes in God*, but unreasonable if one does not.

Protagoras wrote, "Concerning the gods, I have no means of knowing whether they exist or not or of what sort they may be, because of the obscurity of the subject and the brevity of human life."[64] But obscurity and brevity of human life do not mean we can know nothing about the spiritual, the mysterious, the transcendental. The simple ancient argument, said to be stated first by Parmenides, is persuasive.[65] *Ex nihilo, nihil fit.* Of nothing, nothing comes.

Major premise: Something cannot come from nothing.
Minor premise: Here all around us is something, including me, who I know to be a thinking thing.
Conclusion: Something must always have existed.

Some call that "something" that has always existed God. Others call that "something" Brahman, the one, supreme, universal spirit or soul that is the origin and support of the phenomenal universe.[66] Some reject the "something" altogether, but find themselves helpless to refute the logic of *ex nihilo, nihil fit*. By the way, the Big Bang Theory provides no solace, for it merely asserts that something came from nothing, which defies human logic and reasoning.

People who reject the possibility of divine revelation as a way of knowing, or who are agnostic about the possibility of divine revelation, nonetheless, can and do know that murdering, stealing, raping, battering, and lying to defraud are wrong human conduct. They can and do know without appeal to divine revelation, as all rational beings can and do know. Belief in the God of Abraham and divine revelation is not a necessary condition for knowing what moral behavior is, although such belief may be a sufficient reason for many people. Still, either way, by divine revelation or by reasoning alone, everyone knows what right human conduct is—the Moral Imperative—and everyone knows that they know.

—hard to really have your own thoughts

4

Can the Moral Imperative Work?

Morality is of the highest importance—but for us, not for God.

ALBERT EINSTEIN

The Moral Imperative is necessary and sufficient for humans to live together in society with peace, prosperity, and dignity. Without the moral law humans are little more than the fearful creatures Thomas Hobbes described in *Leviathan*, living in a state of "warre," in "… continual fear, and danger of violent death; and the life of man, solitary, poor, nasty, brutish, and short."[67] Hobbes believed that a powerful state—a leviathan—was necessary to keep people from compelling one another, or as Hobbes put it, to "over-awe them all."[68]

But a powerful state is not a good substitute for the moral law. As Lord Acton noted, power corrupts and absolute power corrupts absolutely.[69] If anything, people who comprise "the state" (which is the formidable name given to "government operatives") are sometimes more likely than the rest of us to behave immorally, given the powerful incentives that power over others creates. James Madison wrote in *The Federalist No. 51*, "If men were angels, no government would be necessary."[70] But since men are not angels, a government composed of men will also not be angelic. Respect for the Moral Imperative, especially by people who comprise the state, should be a guiding principle of all statutory law, although such respect is certainly not the case today.

THE MORAL IMPERATIVE IN EVERYDAY LIFE

How would your life and the lives of all people go, if respect for the Moral Imperative were deeply engrained in us all? Imagine a world in which all people avoided compelling others as seriously, carefully, and intently as they avoid falling off 100-foot cliffs. That world is hard to imagine, but let's try.

Makers of locks would be out of business. None of us would consider stealing the property of others, anymore than we would consider chopping off our right hands with an ax. People could and would leave their doors unlocked. Gun makers would be hard pressed for business, too. Shooting another human would be on par with shooting one's self; mostly, people simply would not do it. We would have no fear for our personal safety, since murder, rape, and physical battery would be out of the question, in the very same sense that jumping off 100-foot cliffs is out of the question for most people.

If respect for the Moral Imperative were the supreme value for us all, we would sooner roll in burning embers than compel another unjustly in any way. Slavery? Absurd. We would no more think of enslaving others than we would think of grabbing hold of a 10,000 volt power line while standing in a pool of water. We would no more consider lying to defraud others than we would consider diving headfirst into a tank of boiling oil. The evening news would be merely informative, focused on upcoming events of interest, with occasional, dreadful reports of unfortunate things that have befallen someone, due to what people sometimes call, strangely enough, "acts of God." The intense, voyeuristic, non-stop reporting of people compelling others, and reports of the armies of states (or would-be states) compelling everyone in sight—the staple of today's 24-7-365 news—would be nonexistent, since no one would be compelling anyone.

> *What incentives normal ppl to follow moral imperative if we know others don't. Be moryls?*

Morality

Life lived with unwavering respect for the Moral Imperative may sound ridiculously impossible. Life in the real world could never be that way, we say. But why not? Only because a fairly small number of people—people in both high and low places—do not respect and live by the Moral Imperative. Most people, most of the time, *do* live by the Moral Imperative. Some people *always* live by the Moral Imperative. If everyone did, life on earth would be as close to utopian as life on earth could be. It really is just that simple.

Why do people not chop off their own hand with an ax, not roll in burning embers, not grab hold of 10,000 volt power lines, and not dive headfirst into tanks of boiling oil? They do none of these ghastly acts because most people, most of the time, truly value *their own lives*. If people truly respected and valued the lives of others, and the right of others to be free of compulsion—they would not compel others. It is worth repeating. The Moral Imperative is both necessary and sufficient for humans to live in society with peace, prosperity, and dignity—*do not compel unjustly*.

Tyro: Maybe if I had not had the good luck to be born in America to good middle-class parents, I would be one of those people who steal, cheat, lie, and worse. As some people say, "there but for the grace of God go I."

Solon: Since you speak of a counter-factual hypothetical, Tyro, we cannot say if you would be a moral person aside from your actual circumstances. But we can say that the circumstances of one's birth and rearing do not relieve people of their duty not to compel others.

Tyro: But surly I had an advantage over someone born and raised in poverty.

Solon: The philosopher John Rawls would have agreed with you. He thought life is not fair due to the vagaries and chances of one's birth and rearing.[71] But did you have an advantage? Most people born and raised in poverty behave morally; check your evidence. Only a few people born and raised in poverty behave immorally. A few people born and raised in wealth and advantage also behave immorally; that is the evidence. Moral behavior depends on personal choice and will, not on personal circumstance.

Tyro: Yes, I know, but can we really blame someone for being a thief if he was raised by a family of thieves?

Solon: Yes, Tyro, we most certainly can. Do you not recall how we all come to know that stealing is wrong human conduct—how we can and do know that stealing is wrong? Being raised by a family of thieves does not keep someone from knowing that stealing is wrong.

Tyro: (reflectively) You are right, Solon.

The Moral Imperative is a sufficient prescription for right human behavior in all circumstances that call for moral choice. Acts of stealing, murdering, raping, battering, and enslaving are obviously intentional compulsion by force and therefore immoral. Lying with intent to defraud is also compulsion, although more subtle than aggressive force. Threat of force is tantamount to actual force, and therefore also immoral. Breaking promises may also be compelling another, and therefore wrong behavior for humans, depending on the intentions of the promise breaker. In all circumstances, for any act of moral choice, the Moral Imperative is sufficient to guide rational people away from immoral choices.

Is the Moral Imperative truly a clear, simple, unerring guide to right human conduct? Are there no gray areas? Let's push and shove the Moral Imperative around a bit to explore.

Scenario 1: In the movie *Forrest Gump*, Lt. Dan Taylor begs Forrest to leave him to die on a Vietnamese battlefield. Instead, Forrest throws Lt. Dan over his shoulder and carries him to safety. Did Forrest Gump behave immorally by compelling Lt. Dan?

Lt. Dan was not rational at the time he begged Forest Gump to leave him to die in presumed honor. Indeed, upon regaining his rationality, Lt. Dan thanked Forrest Gump for his act of compulsion. The Moral Imperative written in full form says, "do not intentionally compel another rational being unjustly." Forrest Gump did indeed compel Lt. Dan, but he did not compel a rational Lt. Dan *unjustly*.

Scenario 2: Parents compel children all the time. Are parents therefore behaving immorally?

Not usually. Children are not fully rational. Ordinary compulsion of children by parents to teach, correct, guide, and protect is not a violation of the Moral Imperative. On the other hand, parents who compel their children with intent to harm or disadvantage the children are abusing them, and are therefore behaving immorally. All rational people know the difference.

Scenario 3: Your neighbor is away on vacation. One evening around 10 p.m., you peer out your window and see what you think might be burglars breaking in through the back door of your neighbor's house. You see them carry out a flat-screen T.V. You do not call the police. Is your behavior immoral?

What is your intention? Immoral acts are those intended to harm or disadvantage another. If your failure to call the police is intended to facilitate the burglary, because you wish your neighbor ill, then your inaction is immoral. But if your inaction is due to uncertainty, fear, or even disinterest, then your behavior is moral, though perhaps lacking virtue.

The Moral Imperative prohibits compulsion intended to harm or disadvantage another rational being. You cannot know whether the people carrying out your neighbor's T.V. are burglars or hired moving men. And even if they are burglars, The moral law does not require you to act virtuously. Morality and virtue are not synonyms.

Scenario 4: You are a scratch golfer. An acquaintance at the club, Fred, who you know to be a 15 handicap golfer who likes to gamble challenges you to a match for $100. You decline. Fred persists, calling you a chicken. Fred says he will even play you heads up—no handicap strokes. You finally accept Fred's challenge. Have you behaved immorally?

Electing to accept Fred's lopsided challenge does not compel him; hence, your act is not immoral. It is possible, though entirely unlikely, that Fred could win the match, even playing you heads up with no handicap strokes given. Readers who play golf know such an outcome is not impossible, just highly improbable. Taking advantage of someone you think is a fool is not virtuous, but is also not immoral. Who knows; maybe it is you who are the fool.

On the other hand, if you believe Fred's gambling challenge is more than just persistent bad judgment—a psychological compulsion, say—you would have a moral duty not to gamble with Fred, just as we have a moral duty to care for others who are incapable of rational choice. In this scenario, your intention is important.

Scenario 5: A woman knocks at your door one evening. She has three young children in tow. The woman tells you they are hungry, that she has no money to buy food. You turn them away, telling them that you gave at the office. Have you behaved immorally?

Turning away a starving family is certainly not virtuous in the judgment of most people, but it is also not immoral. Not helping people in obvious need of help epitomizes behavior that is moral but not virtuous.

If it does not compel another unjustly, virtuous behavior is moral behavior, but moral behavior is not necessarily virtuous. Again, morality and virtue are not the same thing. Fortunately, most people who live by the Moral Imperative also behave virtuously. We would be hard pressed to find people who respect the Moral Imperative who would turn away a starving mother and her children. As it happens, most people who behave morally also behave virtuously.

Scenario 6: You are out for a stroll in the park. You come upon a gang of three rather large teenagers slapping and bullying a fourth teenager. You go on your way. Have you behaved immorally?

You have compelled no one unjustly; hence, your behavior is not immoral. Again, the Moral Imperative does not require that people behave virtuously. Perhaps you are fearful that the bullying teenagers will attack you if you intervene. Bravery is a virtue in the minds of many people, and bravery is commendable, but we can behave morally without being virtuous.

If you choose to intervene to stop the bullying, your intervention would not be immoral, even if it requires force or threat of force. The bullying teenagers, through their compulsion of another, forfeit their right to be free of compulsion, by the Principle of Reciprocity. Resisting compulsion on one's own account, or in defense of another, is not an immoral act.

Scenario 7: You are following an old man on a sidewalk in a city. You see a $100 bill fall from the man's pocket. You pick up the bill and place it in your own pocket without a word. Have you behaved immorally?

Your act is a choice that intentionally compels the old man to give you his property. The fact that you did not assault the man to compel him is irrelevant. Your intention to disadvantage the man for your own gain is decisive.

Scenario 8: You are selling your house. You know that your house has a cracked foundation footing, but you do not disclose this information to interested buyers. Have you behaved immorally?

Yes, your silence amounts to lying with intent to defraud or disadvantage another. If you believe that buyers will lose interest if you told them about the cracked foundation, concealing the information is a form of compulsion, though certainly more subtle than overt aggressive force.

Scenario 9: Hansel delights in revealing his private parts to unsuspecting young ladies he encounters in the park. Is Hansel's deviant behavior immoral?

Yes. Hansel's unwelcome behavior compels others to do something they would not otherwise do without Hansel's compulsion; moreover, he knows it. If Hansel asked permission and got it from his potential viewers, his behavior might not be immoral, if the young ladies have reached the age of consent.

Scenario 10: John asks Jill to marry him and Jill promises that she will, after she graduates from college. Upon graduation, Jill tells John she will not marry him. Is Jill's failure to keep her promise immoral?

Breaking a promise to another can be a form of compulsion, depending on the intention of the promise breaker. Several possibilities come to mind. Jill may have made the promise disingenuously in the first place. If she did, she may have been lying with intent to harm or disadvantage. But her lie may have been intended to spare the feelings of John, not to harm or disadvantage him.

Jill may have made the promise of marriage in good faith, but changed her mind by the time graduation arrived. Is Jill morally obligated to keep her promise, even though she no longer wants to marry John? No. If Jill has no desire to harm or disadvantage John, breaking her promise would not meet the necessary condition of intentionality to rise to the level of immorality.

Scenario 11: You sign a contract to sell your car to Sam, with delivery next week. Next week arrives and you decide to keep your car, even though Sam wants to buy it as agreed. Have you behaved immorally?

Breach of contract is intentionally breaking a promise, and is tantamount to stealing. Your contract with Sam gave Sam a property right. Intentionally denying Sam that property right is stealing, which we all know to be immoral.

Scenario 12: You truly believe in good faith that your 25-year old daughter should not marry Harrison, because you have good reason to believe that Harrison is a scoundrel. You tell your daughter that Harrison is a scoundrel and why you think so. She listens to you, but does not agree with you. You then tell your daughter that if she marries Harrison, you will remove her from your will, which presently names her as the beneficiary of your $10 million estate. Your daughter reluctantly turns Harrison down with considerable remorse. You are satisfied that you have done the right thing, because you did it for what you take to be the best interests of your daughter. Have you behaved immorally?

No, your behavior is not immoral. Moreover, you have not compelled your daughter with intent to harm or disadvantage her with force, threat of force, or guile. You offered your daughter a choice, but preserved her right to be free of unjust compulsion.

The hypothetical scenarios above show that what may seem to be gray areas for the Moral Imperative typically involve one or both of two elements: first, the distinction between morality and virtue, and second, the intentions of the actor. Moral philosophers can and do write volumes of casuistic deliberations about the morality or ethics of specific scenarios. But for purposes of this book, such fine distinctions are unnecessary. Deciding whether capitalism is moral or not—which is the purpose of this book— will not require such fine distinctions.

THE MORAL IMPERATIVE AND MORAL DILEMMAS

Some people think that all moral prescriptions are debilitated by shades of gray, are hopelessly ambiguous, are relative, and are circumstantial. People who reject absolute, deontological moral law sometimes offer up moral dilemmas as a case in point against the possibility of any immutable moral law. Although this book is not a treatise on moral philosophy, and certainly does not purport to offer the final word on moral dilemmas, exploring how the Moral Imperative stacks up in the face of purported moral dilemmas may be instructive.

Consider the case of author William Styron's *Sophie's Choice*.[72] Sophie and her two children are imprisoned in a Nazi concentration camp. A guard tells Sophie that one of her children will be allowed to live but one will be killed. The guard tells Sophie she must decide which child will be killed. Sophie can prevent the death of either of her children, but only by condemning the other to death. If she refuses to choose, both will be killed. What will the Moral Imperative have Sophie do?

Or consider the fabled "trolley" dilemma, of which several ethicists have proposed various versions. You are the driver of a runaway trolley tram. You can steer from the track you are on, but to only one other; five men are working on one track and one man on the other; anyone on the track you choose is bound to be killed. What would the Moral Imperative have you do?

Ethicists and others have proposed any number of such purported moral dilemmas, which can be devised seemingly without end.[73] The central feature of so-called moral dilemmas is that a moral agent is required in some proposed circumstance (often rather fanciful) to do either of two mutually exclusive actions; the person must do either of the actions, but cannot do both. The person caught in the moral dilemma seems condemned to moral failure. How does the Moral Imperative fare in the face of such moral dilemmas?

The Moral Imperative fares no better nor worse than any other theory of morality in the face of purported moral dilemmas. The Moral Imperative does not tell Sophie which child to save and which to let die, nor does any other theory of morality. The Moral Imperative does not tell the tram operator which track to choose. Neither the Golden Rule nor Kant's Categorical Imperative will suffice either. Some people who deny the possibility of any absolute moral law take this finding as evidence that the idea of moral behavior is meaningless.

Of course, utilitarianism instructs the tram operator to kill the one to spare the five. But the failures of utilitarianism as a theory of morality are well known. John Rawls wrote his lauded book, *A Theory of Justice*, in part to destroy utterly any notions that utilitarianism has any merit whatsoever as a theory of justice.[74] In that aim, Rawls succeed brilliantly, although his alternative idea of "justice as fairness" is unconvincing to many moral philosophers.

The philosophy of utilitarianism proposes that actions that maximize the sum total of happiness of individuals, counting the happiness of each person equally, are superior and preferred to actions that do not. Attributed to Jeremy Bentham, an 18th century English philosopher, utilitarianism is sometimes summarized as saying that morality and justice consist of doing those things that produce the greatest good for the greatest number. For utilitarianism, it is the sum of happiness that matters, regardless of who in particular is happy. Moreover, the happiness of Annie counts for no more than the happiness of Bobby or Callie per se. But if some act would bring about more happiness for Annie than it produced unhappiness for Bobby and Callie added together, then by all means, that act would be moral and just, according to utilitarianism. In that sense, utilitarianism is egalitarian, placing no importance whatsoever on the happiness of particular individuals.

But as many philosophers have noted, following utilitarian edicts would give us prescriptions that most people simply cannot accept. For example, slavery would be a laudable practice, if only the number of slave owners is greater than the number of slaves, or if the sum of happiness of the slave owners exceeds the unhappiness of the slaves (if slaves happen to outnumber owners). Although some philosophers call utilitarianism a theory of morality and justice, others, such as Peter Kreeft, argue that utilitarianism disavows morality altogether, constituting instead, an amoral proposition for human actions.

Yet, much of what passes for justification of immoral compulsion of people by their governments is the soundly discredited theory of utilitarianism. In that regard, utilitarian philosophy is the bane of the modern world, including America. The idea that immoral means justify what are claimed to be virtuous ends is the justification commonly offered by politicians and other government operatives of all stripes. But if unjust compulsion is the means employed—force, threat of force, or guile—the means are *part of the ends*.

The Moral Imperative tells us not to compel another with intention to harm or disadvantage the other. The hypothetical tram operator lacks intention to harm or disadvantage the people on either track. Consequently, the famous trolley dilemma does not pose a genuine moral dilemma; immoral behavior must be intentional, desired behavior of the actor. The tram operator, and Sophie for that matter, should flip a coin, since no choice based on moral principle is possible, by the Moral Imperative or by any other theory of morality.

The possibility of genuine moral dilemmas is disputed by some philosophers, but of course, other philosophers disagree.[75] Most hypothetical scenarios offered as moral dilemmas are contrived and highly unlikely to occur in the lived world. In any case, for purposes of this book and its two major claims—that capitalism is moral and that capitalism is the only system of political economy that is moral—the possibility of moral dilemmas is unimportant. The Moral Imperative is necessary and sufficient to allow and promote human *eudaimonia*, and the Moral Imperative is also a reliable guide to ethical behavior.

5

Why Be Moral?

Aim above morality. Be not simply good, be good for something.

HENRY DAVID THOREAU[76]

Because humans are rational thinking beings, we understand the Principle of Reciprocity and its logical consequence, the Moral Imperative. Imperatives are commands; "go home;" "shut up;" "run fast;" "do not compel." The Moral Imperative *commands* us not to compel others. Commands imply commanders; who is the commander of the Moral Imperative? Why should we obey the Moral Imperative? Why be moral?

For some people, the God of Abraham is the commander. For people of faith, the answer to the question "why be moral?" is entirely obvious. God-fearing people *should* do what God says—always, no excuses, without fail—notwithstanding the observable evidence that some do not. But what about people who do not believe in the God of Abraham? Who is the commander of the Moral Imperative for people who do not believe in the God of Abraham?

Tyro: I know that stealing is wrong, irrational behavior. But why should I care? Why shouldn't I steal, if stealing will get me what I want?

Solon: What an interesting question, Tyro. How do we get to a statement of "should" from a statement of what "is"? Moral behavior *is* right behavior for humans, but why *should* we behave rightly?

Tyro: The words "should" and "ought" seem to imply some goal, objective, or purpose, don't they?

Solon: Just so, Tyro. The words "should" and "ought" plead for an answer to the question "why." For what purpose. Statements that include "should" or "ought" are normative statements—statements about someone's values—unless they also include an "if" clause.

Tyro: So, I *should* do something only *if* I think that doing that something will promote my goal or purpose?

Solon: Why else would a rational person do anything?

MORALITY AND RECIPROCITY

People can know the moral law by thinking alone, because humans are rational beings who understand the Principle of Reciprocity. If I have a right to be free of compulsion from others, then others must have an obligation not to compel me. Rights without obligations are quite impossible. If I have the right not to be compelled, others also have that right, which means I have an obligation to others. That idea is the Principle of Reciprocity.

But knowing that compelling others is irrational behavior does not tell us why we should not compel—unless we believe that we *must* behave rationally. Why not steal if we can get away with it without punishment? What if we just want something that is not ours? Why not rape someone if we want to, if we could do so without punishment? Why not assault and batter those who get in our way or offend us? Why not cheat others, defrauding them with lies that result in our own benefit? *Must* we behave rationally? Clearly, humans do not have to behave rationally, and some people do not.

Immanuel Kant tells us we are duty-bound to behave morally. But if we are duty-bound, we must be bound by duty *to someone*. Kant thought that each of us is obligated to ourselves alone. For Kant, we are duty-bound to behave morally even in Onesville. But how can one have a duty to one's self? One simply *is* one's self. If we have a duty to be moral, we have that duty *to others*. By the Principle of Reciprocity, each of us does have a duty not to compel others, *if we believe that we ourselves have a right not to be compelled by others*. Notice the "if" clause. From the Principle of Reciprocity we can get a "should" statement, but only with the help of an "if" clause. We should behave morally, *if* we believe we must behave rationally. Put in the form of a syllogism,

Major premise: people must behave rationally.
Minor premise: *not compelling others is rational behavior.*
Conclusion: *people must not compel others.*

The syllogism is valid, since its conclusion is entailed by its premises. If we want to attack a valid syllogism, we must attack its premises. Compelling others is irrational behavior, and not compelling others unjustly is rational behavior. But *must* humans behave rationally? Perhaps not. The major premise of the syllogism may be suspect. Can we think of a reason that humans *must* behave rationally? Perhaps not, but like Plato, we can believe that people do behave rationally, *if they know—really know—what is good for them*; rational behavior is a fundamental feature of human nature.

So, we are back where we started. Why should we behave morally? As with all other "should" statements, we should behave morally *if we want to achieve some desired result*. We can identify at least three widely prevalent human values that constitute powerful "if" clauses for commanding one's self to obey the Moral Imperative—virtue, freedom, and social cooperation. Kant is right; in the end, each rational individual is and must be one's own commander of the Moral Imperative. But the commander will require reasons.

MORALITY AND VIRTUE

Virtue is chosen, praiseworthy, habitual behavior. Praise comes to us from others; consequently, virtuous behavior is behavior that others approve.

What we call virtue depends on behaviors that humans value. People are said to be virtuous if they routinely choose praiseworthy behavior. Annie is courageous, if she routinely chooses courageous behavior in the face of danger. Bobby is honest, if he routinely refuses to dissemble. Callie is patient, if she routinely refuses to be angry or frustrated with her own failures or with the failures of Annie and Bobby.

The meaning of the words "right" and "wrong" depends on rationality and reason. In contrast, the meaning of the words "good" and "bad" depends on what humans value. We can know by thinking alone that compelling others unjustly is *wrong* behavior, but does that knowledge make compelling others *bad* behavior, and therefore reprehensible? We know that not compelling others is *right* behavior, but is it *good* behavior, and therefore praiseworthy behavior?

Tyro: What does it mean to be "good"?

Solon: What do you think, Tyro?

Tyro: I think the meaning of the word "good" depends on who you ask.

Solon: If so, Tyro, that would mean the word "good" really has no particular meaning at all.

Tyro: Maybe it doesn't. Maybe nothing is really good or bad.

Solon: Some people make that claim, but their actions and words show plainly that they do not really believe that nothing is really good or bad.

Tyro: What do you mean?

Solon: People praise what they take to be good and condemn what they take to be bad. Do you know anyone who does not praise and condemn?

Tyro: No, not really. Everyone I have ever known both praises and condemns the actions of other people.

Solon: Just so, Tyro. People praise behavior they value and condemn behavior they do not value.

Tyro: But doesn't that fact leave it up to each individual to determine what is praiseworthy and blameworthy, since value is subjective and individual?

Solon: Definitely, Tyro.

Tyro: So, doesn't that mean that nothing is *really* good or bad?

Solon: I do not think so.

Tyro: I am very confused.

Solon: The word "good" has meaning only in the context of "good for something." The expression "be good" has no meaning as an abstraction. Contrary to popular belief, and the theme of countless literary works of art, good and bad are not existents, not part of reality.

Tyro: I'm not sure I understand what you mean.

Solon: What is a good knife?

Tyro: The purpose of a knife is cutting; a good knife cuts well.

Solon: Just so, Tyro. And a bad knife cuts poorly. The "something" that a knife can be good or bad for is cutting.

Tyro: Okay; I see what you mean by "good for something." So, what does it mean to say that someone is good or bad?

Solon: Saying that someone is good or bad strikes me as confused language, Tyro. People themselves are neither good nor bad; it is the behavior of people that can be good or bad or neither, and then only if the behavior is good, bad, or neither for some purpose.

Tyro: But people do say things like "Bobby is a bad man;" "Annie is a good women," do they not?

Solon: Some people say such things; some do not. I do not.

Tyro: Why not?

Solon: What would it mean to say "Bobby is a bad man"?

Tyro: I guess it would mean that Bobby does bad things.

Solon: Such as?

Tyro: Suppose Bobby stole my iPod. That would be bad behavior, wouldn't it?

Solon: Stealing your iPod would be wrong, immoral behavior, just as the Moral Imperative tells us. But why would it be bad behavior?

Tyro: It would be bad behavior because I don't like it.

Solon: Stealing your iPod is bad behavior because you do not value such behavior, which is a value that most people seem to share, by the way.

Tyro: Okay. I see what you mean. Stealing my iPod might be good for the purpose of bringing the thief immediate psychic satisfaction, but bad for the purpose of bringing me value. But stealing is immoral behavior for everyone.

Solon: Excellent, Tyro! The words "good" and "bad" are descriptors that depend for meaning on what someone values. The words "right" and "wrong" are descriptors of action that depend on rationality and reason.

---

why isn't the right thing always good?

Moral behavior is right behavior; virtuous behavior is good behavior. Moral behavior—behavior that does not compel others unjustly—may be good, bad, or neither, but moral behavior is always right behavior. Good behavior is good only if it is good for something. Consequently, we can conceive of behavior that is good, better, or best. We cannot conceive of behavior that is right, righter, or rightest. Virtue admits to degrees; morality does not. My behavior may be thought by others to be good, if I give money to St. Jude's hospital for children. Your behavior may be thought by others to be even better, if you always act moderately and prudently. Mother Teresa's behavior might be thought by some people to be best, if she devoted all her actions to helping others.

We should be moral, if we want to be virtuous. This book began with the claim that most people want to be good. People really do want to be good people. Even those people who don't want to be good people solely for the value of being virtuous alone, still want others to believe they are good people. But moral behavior is a necessary condition for being virtuous. We cannot be virtuous if we are not first moral. Consequently, if we want to be virtuous, we *should* be moral. People who want to be virtuous *should* obey the Moral Imperative.

MORALITY AND FREEDOM

[handwritten note: what if someone chooses moral behavior for you]

Believing that we are free to choose our actions is a necessary condition for moral behavior. For if we are not free to choose our behavior—or as Kant said, at least believe that we are free to choose—the concept of moral behavior is vacuous and meaningless. Without freedom to choose, humans would be like rocks, behaving as rocks do, only according to the natural laws that describe the inanimate, soulless (or mindless, if you prefer) behavior of matter and energy in time. But again following Kant, moral behavior, which is behavior that conforms to the Moral Imperative, is necessary for humans to be free. Kant wrote, "We have finally reduced the definite conception of morality to the idea of freedom."[77] We cannot be free if we do not behave morally.

The words "freedom," "power," and "will" have interdependent meanings. One cannot exercise will if one is not free to act; hence, will and freedom are bound up together in humans. One who has no power to act also has no freedom; hence, power and freedom are codependent. One who is forced by another to act is denied will by force; hence, will and power are interdependent. In the end, freedom, power, and will are virtually indistinguishable.

Tyro: I think that whoever stole my iPod does not deserve to be free.
Solon: According to Kant, whoever stole your iPod is free to choose, but not really free.
Tyro: (with a puzzled expression on his face) How so?
Solon: Kant thought that to be free, people must choose their actions by a good will alone. Stealing your iPod could not possibly be an

action directed by the thief's good will. Whoever stole your iPod must have done so for some reason other than the choice of his own good will. Consequently, the thief was not really free. The thief was driven by something outside his own good will.

Tyro: Do you mean the thief was somehow not free to choose?

Solon: The thief was free to choose and did so. The thief had the power to steal your iPod and the will to do so, but evidently had some motivation other than a good will to do so. Kant would say the thief was not free, since the act of stealing was motivated by some desire other than good will.

Tyro: I must admit that I don't quite get what Kant had in mind.

Solon: You would not be alone in that regard.

Tyro: I can see that stealing is compelling and that compelling denies others freedom. I can see that if everyone is a thief, no one can be free. I can see that since I *do* want to be free, I don't want everyone to be a thief. I can see that if I don't want everyone to be a thief, I should not be a thief myself.

Solon: You see much, Tyro. And I think that all rational beings can and do see what you see.

Most people want to be free. Freedom is a nearly universal human value. But we cannot be free if we are compelled by others. Consequently, if we want to be free, we *should* be moral. People who want to be free *should* obey the Moral Imperative.

MORALITY AND SOCIAL COOPERATION

To state the obvious, we are not alone. For better or worse, we live among others, comprising together a society. Why and how societies and their governments come about have been fascinating questions for many philosophers, including Plato, Aristotle, John Locke, Thomas Hobbes, Jean-Jacques Rousseau, Lewis Henry Morgan, Adam Smith, Karl Marx,

Frederick Engels, Sigmund Freud, and more recently John Rawls and Robert Nozick—to name but a few. But regardless of the theories these and other writers proposed, all agree that social cooperation is desirable and beneficial for humans. For without cooperation among the individuals who comprise society, life as humans on earth will indeed be solitary, poor, nasty, brutish, and short, just as Hobbes said.

But we must take care when we use the word "society" and its derivatives, for society is nothing more than an abstract, collective noun. Society does not exist; society is nothing more than the name of a set of individuals. Political borders pretend to define the boundaries of a society, but of course they do not, because a society is not an existent. Society has no mind; only individuals have minds. Society cannot choose; only individuals choose. Society does not have values; only individuals have values. If we begin to think of society as something more than a collection of individuals, we run the risk of thinking that a collection of individuals has greater meaning, value, and importance than individuals.

Sadly enough, the sloppy habit of anthropomorphizing the abstract concept of society is an egregious mental error that leads to immoral acts in the name of doing good. Language that speaks of "social justice," "the social good," "social values," "social needs," "social welfare," and "social choice" will likely mislead more than enlighten.

Tyro: Shouldn't we be moral for the good of society?
Solon: What do you mean by "the good of society," and why would anyone care about society?
Tyro: The good of society is whatever is good for everyone.
Solon: Can you give me an example of something that is good for everyone?
Tyro: Yes. Food is good for everyone.
Solon: What do you mean by "food"?
Tyro: That's silly, Solon. Everyone knows what food is.

Solon: Since everyone knows, you will have no trouble telling me.
Tyro: Food is stuff we eat.
Solon: Is that so? "We" do not eat anything. I may eat something; you may eat something; we might both even eat the same thing. But "we" do not eat anything.
Tyro: You know what I mean, Solon.
Solon: On the contrary, I do not know what you mean. Moreover, I do not think you know what you mean. Back to my question; can you give me an example of something that is good for everyone?
Tyro: I think you are playing semantic games.
Solon: That notion is a common refuge of people who say things that have no meaning—things like "the good of society." By the way, the word "semantic" refers to the meaning of words. We are definitely talking about semantics, but it is not a game.
Tyro: (with a bit of exasperation) Isn't moral behavior, as stipulated by the Moral Imperative, good for everyone?
Solon: Whoever stole your iPod did not behave morally, but may be enjoying your iPod right now. We could say that not behaving morally was good for the thief, could we not? Would not stealing your iPod have been good for the thief?
Tyro: (with a pleased expression on his face) I get it. What you're trying to get me to see is that whatever is good, is good for an individual, not for everyone.
Solon: Just so, Tyro! The distinction may seem unimportant or trivial, but it is not. Social cooperation is about people agreeing about interacting *as individuals*, not about individuals somehow being all the same, valuing the same things, or valuing the same things equally.

Social cooperation is beneficial and desired by all rational people. We intuitively understand that our lives are enriched and improved by our voluntary interactions with others. The power of social interaction through the division of labor is one of the most profound and important insights offered by Adam Smith in his most celebrated book, *An Inquiry into the Nature and Causes of the Wealth of Nations*.[78] In his rather neglected, but exceptional book, *Theory and History*, Ludwig von Mises further explains the power of social cooperation brilliantly.[79] But how will it be possible for millions of individuals—each with individual minds, preferences, and values—to cooperate? The only feasible answer is by behaving morally. Consequently, if we want the benefits of social cooperation, we *should* be moral. People who want to live together in a society *should* obey the Moral Imperative.

The philosopher David Hume argued famously that we cannot derive an "ought" from an "is." Hume's observation is known these days as the "is-ought gap," "Hume's Law," or "Hume's Guillotine."[80] But we can conclude with an "ought" from an "is," with the aid of an "if." All rational beings know the moral law and agree that the moral law—as expressed by the Moral Imperative—*is* right behavior for humans. All rational beings who want to be virtuous, free, and social people *should* obey the moral law.

Part II: Capitalism

In a capitalist society, all human relationships are voluntary. Men are free to cooperate or not, to deal with one another or not, as their own individual judgments, convictions, and interests dictate. They can deal with one another only in terms of and by means of reason, i.e., by means of discussion, persuasion, and contractual agreement, by voluntary choice to mutual benefit.

Ayn Rand[81]

6

What Is Capitalism?

Capitalism is what people do when you leave them alone.

KENNETH MINOGUE[82]

Tyro: Solon, I am puzzled.

Solon: That is a good thing, Tyro. Puzzlement is the beginning of wisdom. What is it that puzzles you?

Tyro: Today in school, our history teacher told us that some guy named Karl Marx wrote that capitalism is just a temporary evolutionary stage in human history that empowers the wealthy, exploits the working class, and keeps them poor. He also told us that socialism will eventually replace capitalism.

Solon: Why does that puzzle you, Tyro?

Tyro: Because our teacher also told us that America is a capitalist country. But most people in America are certainly not poor. It seems to me that America is one of the richest countries in the world, and that lots of other countries that are not anything like capitalist countries *do* have lots of poor people.

Solon: Perhaps your teacher does not know what capitalism really is.

Capitalism is a social system of political economy. In the words of Ayn Rand,

> [A] social system is a set of moral-political-economic principles embodied in a society's laws, institutions, and government, which determine the relationships, the terms of association, among the men living in a given geographical area. ... Capitalism is a social system based on the recognition of individual rights, including property rights, in which all property is privately owned.[83]

Milton Friedman, the preeminent Nobel laureate and defender of capitalism, offered the following description of capitalism:

> A working model of a society organized through voluntary exchange, is a free private enterprise exchange economy—what we have been calling competitive capitalism.[84]

Tens, if not hundreds of writers have proposed definitions and descriptions of capitalism.[85] But in the end, the four essential, defining elements of capitalism are private property, voluntary exchange, freedom, and just law. To understand what capitalism is—what it really is and what it is not—we must explore the genesis, meaning, and implications of these four foundational elements of capitalism.

PRIVATE PROPERTY

What does it mean to own property? What can someone own? How does anyone come to own anything in the first place? If we all agree that Callie owns something today, how can Annie or Bobby come to own that same property tomorrow?

Tyro: I know what it means to own something. I used to own an iPod, but someone stole it from me.

Solon: Indeed, Tyro. We would have no meaning for stealing without first having a meaning for private property. What do you think it means to own something?

Tyro: Owning something means it's mine and that I have property rights.

Solon: What does it mean to say something is yours, Tyro? What rights do you think owning something gives you?

Tyro: If something is mine, that means I have the right to do with it whatever I want.

Solon: Is that so? If you own a car, would that mean you have a right to drive it at 120 miles per hour through town?

Tyro: Of course not.

Solon: So, owning property does not appear to mean that you have the right to do with it *whatever* you want.

Tyro: Okay; I see your point. But I would have property rights. I would have the right to use my car any way I chose that did not harm other people. I would have the right to use my car, sell it to someone, or even give it away, if I wanted to.

Solon: I think you and every other person has but one fundamental right; we each have the right to be free of unjust compulsion from others. If that proposition is true, what would it mean to say you have property rights?

Tyro: If our only right is to be free of compulsion from others, then the only property right I could have is that others have no right to compel me to use my property in any particular way, or to interfere with how I choose to use my property, so long as I do not compel others.

Solon: Excellent, Tyro! What we commonly call property rights are really limitations on what others can do, just as James Sadowsky wrote in his essay, *Private Property and Collective Ownership*.[86]

What it means to own property is deeply engrained in each of us. All people know what private property is, because we each own some—ourselves. The idea of self ownership, which is so fundamental that it seems entirely self evident, is sometimes attributed to John Locke, who wrote,

> *Though the earth and all inferior creatures be common to all men, yet every man has a "property" in his own "person." This nobody has any right to but himself.*[87]

We all agree with Locke. Just as surely as you know you own yourself, so do all people know that they also own themselves.

Yet, ownership of one's self has not always been honored in statutory law. Slavery, as a legal institution of one human owning another human, has been a common practice throughout ancient and modern history around the world. Sadly enough, even the original United States Constitution, the supreme law of America, held that a human could be owned by another. Not until the late 20th Century did slavery acquire its now universal condemnation in statutory law. How very strange that such a fundamental principle in natural law would require such a long time in human history to become universally proclaimed in codified law.

Most people, also following Locke's theory of property, agree that individuals naturally own the product of their own labor. Locke wrote,

> *The "labour" of his body and the "work" of his hands, we may say, are properly his. Whatsoever, then, he removes out of the state that Nature hath provided and left it in, he hath mixed his labour with it, and joined to it something that is his own, and thereby makes it his property.*[88]

But very little can be produced by labor alone, save perhaps a few elementary services. Production of even simple services requires use of land, if for nothing more than a place to stand. Production of goods and services typically requires all three categories of scarce resources; notably, what economists call land, labor and capital. As a shorthand, following the terminology of classical economics, let us call all naturally occurring, non-living, non-human resources "land." Tools, machinery, buildings, and other such physical co-agents of production, which are not naturally occurring, but must themselves be produced by humans, we will call "capital."

According to Murray Rothbard, ownership of one's self is the foundation of private property of any kind, including land.[89] For if one did not own one's self—if someone else somehow did, instead—then the whole idea of ownership of any kind of property would be self-detonating, self-contradictory, unintelligible, and meaningless. For if one does not own one's self, then others would also not own themselves, by the Principle of Reciprocity and ontological equality. The proposition that one does not own one's self degenerates into an infinite regress in which no one owns anything. Rothbard's argument is interesting logically, but unnecessary, since *every* human agrees that we each are the sole owners of ourselves. People also agree that we each are the sole property owners of whatever we produce ourselves (perhaps with voluntary, contracted assistance from others). But what about private property in land?

Even if we all agree that we each own ourselves and the products of our own labor, that leaves open the question of who could and should own "land"—not just terra firma itself, but minerals found naturally in the earth, the spontaneous fruits of nature, ground water, rivers, the oceans of the earth, the atmosphere, and so on. How is it that a particular person comes to own land? A broadly agreed answer to that question is essential for a workable political economy.

—∞—

Tyro: Our sociology teacher told us that in an ideal society land would be owned collectively. Individuals would not and could not own land.

Solon: Did he really? How interesting. If no one owned land, how would people sort out who controls the use of land and who would own the goods and services people produce using land?

Tyro: He said that Karl Marx solved that problem with the maxim "from each according to his ability, to each according to his need."[90]

Solon: And what do you think of that Marxian maxim, Tyro?

Tyro: Well, I'm not sure it's clear who would decide what anyone needs or how anyone would know who is able to provide what some other person needs. And why would someone who does happen to be able to produce something be willing to produce it for someone else?

Solon: Perhaps Marx did not think carefully about those questions. In any case, some *one person*, or some very small committee of persons, always owns particular land; otherwise, the land is not owned at all. Collective ownership of land is a naive notion that is impractical and not really possible in practice.

Tyro: Why do you say that collective ownership of land is not really possible?

Solon: Can you say that you own property that you do not and cannot yourself control? Do you own property that you cannot use as you yourself choose? Do you really own property that you cannot sell to another, if you chose to do so?

Tyro: No, I guess not. Not really.

Solon: You guess correctly, Tyro. In all societies and in all times, some *particular* person, or perhaps some very small committee of persons (which committee is usually dominated by some one person), always controls the use and disposition of *particular* land; otherwise, that particular land is not yet owned. The person who *controls* the use of land is the de facto owner of the property, regardless of any legal or nominal distinctions that someone might like to make to the contrary.

Tyro: What about public property? Don't governments own land in the name of the people as public property? What about public roads? What about the oceans? What about national parks?

Solon: Good questions, Tyro. Still, in every case, someone controls the use and disposition of so-called "public property." Just because that someone happened to be elected by majority rule, or perhaps was appointed by some elected politician, does not alter the meaningful statement that the real owner of land is whoever can and does control the use and disposition of so-called public property. Calling roads, national parks, and other land controlled by a government "public property" is more an obfuscation of who the true owner is than a meaningful declaration.

Tyro: But don't we all get to use public roads and other kinds of public property?

Solon: Sometimes—at least until some of us, or all of us, are not allowed to do so by the true owner. Recall what happened to public air space and airports, following the villainous attacks on 9-11. Government operatives can and do declare roads closed as they choose. You and I are not allowed to "trespass" on real estate claimed by the federal government as "government property," but "authorized" persons can. Governments sometimes blockade free and open passage even of the oceans. Operators of national parks charge admission and close their gates as they choose. All land is either unowned or owned. All land that is owned is owned by someone. Whoever controls the use and disposition of land is the true owner.

Tyro: So, we should quit using the term "public property"?

Solon: No, Tyro. That would be impractical. It is fine to call certain land "public property," provided we understand that such property is not and cannot be owned "collectively."

The Homestead Principle posits that a person gains just ownership of *previously unowned* land by performing "acts of original appropriation." Acts of original appropriation include using land productively (e.g., cutting trees on unowned land and making lumber; mining ore found in unowned land and making iron), marking the land (e.g., fencing in land; writing coordinates of land in a register), or joining the land with something one already owns (e.g., building a house on previously unowned land; building a dock on the bank of a previously unowned pond).

For John Locke, mixing one's labor with previously unowned land is an act of original appropriation that establishes original ownership justly. Merely declaring ownership is manifestly insufficient, notwithstanding the arrogant practice of long-dead European kings. In accord with the ideas of Locke, Murray Rothbard also proposed that a person comes to own land by "mixing" one's labor with the land, which land would then become one's property. Rothbard writes in *Man, Economy, and State*,

> ... the origin of all property is ultimately traceable to the appropriation of an unused nature-given factor by a man and his "mixing" his labor with this natural factor to produce a capital good or a consumers' good. For when we trace back through gifts and through exchanges, we must reach a man and an unowned natural resource. In a free society, any piece of nature that has never been used is unowned and is subject to a man's ownership through his first use or mixing of his labor with this resource.[91]

For Rothbard, claims of original ownership of natural resources based on any premise other than first use (by "mixing" one's labor with the land to produce either capital goods or consumption goods) are bogus.[92]

Yet, other philosophers, including Robert Nozick, question the notion of "mixing" one's labor with land as a criterion for justly vesting original ownership of land. In *Anarchy, State, and Utopia*, Nozick devotes several paragraphs to raising fascinating and important questions about Locke's principle of original acquisition. For example, Nozick writes,

> *If I own a can of tomato juice and spill it in the sea so that its molecules (made radioactive, so I can check this) mingle evenly throughout the sea, do I thereby come to own the sea, or have I foolishly dissipated my tomato juice?*[93]

Nozick did not propose an alternative principle for "just acquisition of land." But he did give us the important insight that it is not only persons favoring private property who need a theory of how property rights to land originate justly. People who think the earth is (or should be) owned collectively—such as proponents of Georgism—also share the burden of producing a theory of how persons living in a particular area come to own a particular territory *jointly*. Nozick writes,

> [people who believe in collective ownership of land] also must provide a theory of how such property rights arise; they must show why the persons living there have rights to determine what is done with the land and resources there that persons living elsewhere don't have.[94]

No one has produced a viable alternative to the Homestead Principle, although many philosophers and political thinkers have proposed that land should not be owned, or that land, if owned at all, should be owned collectively. Opponents of private ownership of land are unable to propose workable schemes for using land (which is clearly necessary for human survival) that do not amount to control and disposition of land by *someone*. Whoever that *someone* is, is the de facto owner of the land, to the exclusion of all others.

Anthony de Jasay and Hans-Hermann Hoppe argue that denial of the Homestead Principle is self contradictory, since such denial presupposes a prior ownership claim. Anthony de Jasay writes,

> *The opponent of this simple thesis (the Homestead Principle) is trying to have it both ways: he is both asserting that the thing*

> *(land) has no legitimate first owner from whom a second or nth owner could have legitimately obtained it by agreed transfer, and that there is nevertheless somebody who has been and still is entitled to use the thing (land) and therefore can validly object to being excluded from it.*[95]

Hans-Hermann Hoppe goes a step further, arguing that denial of the Homestead Principle would also contradict the principle of self ownership. Hoppe writes,

> *... it (denial of the Homestead Principle) would be incompatible with the already justified [principle of] self-ownership, for if one could appropriate resources by decree, this would imply that one could also declare another person's body to be one's own.*[96]

Tyro: I think it is beyond dispute that we each own ourselves and the things we ourselves create. But I am having a harder time with private ownership of real estate and other natural resources.

Solon: How so, Tyro?

Tyro: We each are born on earth through no choice of our own, into circumstances we did not choose. Surely we each have a birthright to the earth itself and its naturally occurring resources, don't we?

Solon: People who count themselves as Georgists are proponents of that very theory, Tyro. Henry George argued in *Progress and Poverty*[97] that land and every naturally occurring thing found in nature belong to all of humanity.

Tyro: I like that idea, Solon. I think I may be a Georgist.

Solon: You, Tyro, are a naturally occurring thing found in nature. Do you belong to all of humanity?

Tyro: Okay. So I'm not a Georgist.

What Is Capitalism?

Given that the idea of collective ownership of land is utterly impractical, and in the lived world of practice, an obfuscation of the de facto owner (the person who controls the land), and given that we each definitely own ourselves, must we not agree with Locke, Rothbard, de Jasay, and Hoppe? The Homestead Principle appears to be the only just principle for original acquisition of land. A person comes justly to own previously unowned land by being the first to *mark* and *use* previously unowned land.

Marking land as owned is a necessary condition for homesteading. For unmarked land appears to others to be unowned, and therefore others may rightly think the land remains available for homesteading. In Threesville, suppose Bobby sees a lovely meadow, which he decides to homestead, thereby making it his private property. Callie visits the next day and sees Bobby erecting a fence around the meadow. Callie tells Bobby the meadow belongs to her, unmarked by her for ownership though it is. Now what? Evidently, not marking adds up to not homesteading, and therefore, not meeting a necessary condition for original acquisition of land. Had Callie somehow marked the meadow clearly, in a way that Bobby and Annie agreed constituted marking, Callie would have established original ownership, but without some kind of marking, she did not.

Using land—what Locke and Rothbard called "mixing" one's labor with land—may imply ownership, but without somehow marking the land, use alone leaves others unaware of the extent of claimed ownership. In Threesville, suppose Annie plants a garden on a small patch of previously unowned land, thereby mixing her labor with the land. But without further unambiguous marking, Bobby and Callie would not know that Annie takes herself to be homesteading an entire square mile of land that surrounds her garden. Just as Nozick and others have argued, the act of "mixing" one's labor with land is too ambiguous by itself to constitute a sufficient act of original acquisition.

Marking is a necessary condition for homesteading land, but is marking by itself sufficient to establish a homesteading claim? Can Callie simply mark a plot of unowned land, say by building a fence around it, but use the land in no obvious way further, and thereby acquire the previously unowned land, in accord with the Homestead Principle? Marking alone is both necessary and sufficient to *acquire* unowned land originally. But using land, in the common parlance of what constitutes "use," may not be a necessary condition for homesteading. What if Callie wants to own a natural habitat to preserve it indefinitely in Threesville—just for the value it gives her of knowing the habitat is preserved? Can Callie simply fence in a parcel of land, leaving it in its natural state with no further use, and thereby retain ownership until she voluntarily transfers ownership to Bobby or Annie?

Like Locke, Rothbard proposed that homesteading requires initial use ("mixing" one's labor with the land), and that land acquired by homesteading remains the property of the original homesteader until the land is transferred voluntarily, regardless of whether the homesteader *continues* to use the land.[98] But what if the fence Callie builds to mark her land deteriorates, leaving the land unmarked. Is the land now available for homesteading by Bobby or Annie? Would Callie have abandoned the land and lost ownership of it by allowing the fence to deteriorate? We can see that private ownership of land, though necessary for human survival, is not an easy, straightforward social institution. Nonetheless, private ownership of land is pervasive throughout human history. As Ludwig von Mises wrote in *Human Action*, "if history could teach us anything, it would be that private property is inextricably linked with civilization."[99]

The Homestead Principle appears to be the only rational principle of justice in acquisition, but to make the Homestead Principle practical and operational, members of a society must agree to rules (laws) about what constitutes "marking" and "using" previously unowned land. Will digging a hole in the land constitute using the land? Maybe. Can Bobby declare that he owns Threesville's moon; would that declaration be a sufficient mark, given that the moon is well defined as a visible whole? Probably not. Can Annie "mark" a plot of land by registering latitude and longitude coordinates with a duly constituted government agency? Perhaps. Today's technology suggests possibilities for marking land that would have been impossible a century ago (photographs taken from space). But merely recording coordinates might seem akin to simply declaring ownership, like arrogant kings of old were wont to do. Clearly unacceptable. Bobby cannot simply declare that he owns Annie; neither can he simply declare that he owns some particular previously unowned land in Threesville.

Ultimately, people living together in a society must and do answer these and other questions about what constitutes *legal* and *just* "marking" and "using" to homestead land. People do so through the institutions that comprise their society's political economy, which includes its legal system. Indeed, societies around the globe have done so throughout human history.

We would be hard-pressed today to identify real estate on earth that remains free of an original claim of ownership. For most practical purposes, all real estate on earth has already been homesteaded. Sovereign governments claim ownership even of parts of oceans. It no longer matters much (at least on planet earth) how real estate came originally to be owned privately. What matters much more today is how ownership of land may be transferred justly from its current owner to its next owner.

Nozick explored the question of just transfer of property exhaustively in *Anarchy, State, and Utopia*, summing up with these words:

> *From each according to what he chooses to do, to each according to what he makes for himself (perhaps with the contracted aid of others) and what others choose to do for him and choose to give him of what they've been given previously (under this maxim) and haven't yet expended or transferred.*[100]

Admitting that these words made for an unwieldy maxim (and certainly less than memorable), Nozick offered this pithier version: "From each as they choose, to each as they are chosen."[101] Put plainly, Nozick argued (as have many other philosophers) that voluntary exchange is the only *just* principle of transfer of ownership, including transfer of ownership of land.

Tyro: The Homestead Principle is reasonable, Solon. Still, homesteading seems to place great importance on being first. What's so special about being first?

Solon: Only that first is more special than being second, Tyro. By what reason would a late comer have a superior claim over and above the *first* homesteader?

Tyro: Hmmm. I see what you mean.

Land and labor are the minimally necessary ingredients for producing goods and services that people want. Capital goods, although not absolutely necessary for production, vastly magnify the ability of humans to produce consumer goods. Without tools, machinery, trucks, buildings, roads, bridges, computers, and the technology embodied in such capital goods, human productive power is meager, capable only of the grinding, harsh poverty that was a universal and ordinary condition of nearly all humans as recently as 250 years ago. But human productivity wanes without *privately* owned land, labor and capital. All of history demonstrates the truth of that positive statement.[102,103]

Understanding why private property is essential for human prosperity dates at least as far back in time as Aristotle, who argued convincingly and well against the ideal polis proposed in Plato's *Republic,* a polis that featured communal ownership of land, instead of private property.[104] Foreshadowing Garrett Hardin's explanation in *Tragedy of the Commons*[105] of why communally owned property fails, Aristotle pointed out that resources owned collectively are not as productive as resources owned privately, because people give their greatest attention, interest and care to what they own privately. Communal property also breeds discontent, as some complain that others receive more than they deserve, while contributing too little to the store of communally owned goods. Private property, Aristotle argued further, is in our human nature. We delight in what we own. He also noted that private property has existed everywhere and always in human experience. To conclude his rejection of Plato's proposed communism, Aristotle argued that without private property people have no opportunity to be virtuous by engaging in benevolence and philanthropy. One cannot give to others what one does not own.

Private property is a necessary, foundational, and defining element of capitalism. A system of political economy that is not based on private property, simply is not capitalism. Moreover, without private property, no one would own anything to exchange with others, which leads us to the second essential and defining element of capitalism.

VOLUNTARY EXCHANGE

Adam Smith wrote in *The Wealth of Nations* that "man has almost constant occasion for the help of his brethren."[106] If people were independent, solitary creatures, relying entirely on themselves to produce the goods and services they want, few people could enjoy more than a paltry, subsistence level of life. Among Adam Smith's most important insights is his explanation that specialization in performing particular productive tasks and division of labor (dividing productive activity into several discrete subtasks, in which different individuals specialize) are the foundation and wellspring of vastly expanded capability of humans to produce valuable goods and services.

Comparative advantage (a technical term of economics) among people in performing productive tasks gives rise to specialization, division of labor, and voluntary exchange. In Threesville, Annie, Bobby, and Callie will find that each has a comparative advantage in performing particular physical and mental tasks. Even though Annie is more talented and possesses greater physical and mental skills than Callie in every dimension, Callie will still have what economists call a comparative advantage in performing some tasks. Callie's comparative advantage will provide an avenue for specialization, allowing her to produce some goods or services of value, which she can then trade to Annie and Bobby for other goods she wants, goods which Annie or Bobby specialize in producing.

Readers who do not like detailed numerical examples should skip this paragraph and the next two. As an example of comparative advantage, suppose Annie can catch 20 fish per day, hoe 4 acres of corn per day, or spend her productive efforts doing some of each task. Callie, due to physical and mental limitations endowed by her genes, can catch only 16 fish per day, hoe only 2 acres of corn per day, or do some of each. Annie is more capable and talented in producing both caught fish and hoed corn. But as it happens, Callie has a comparative advantage over Annie in fishing, and Annie has a comparative advantage over Callie in hoeing corn.

The cost of hoeing an acre of corn is 5 fish for Annie (cost correctly reckoned is value that must be given up when people choose one action over another). That's because Annie must give up 5 fish if she chooses to use her time hoeing an acre of corn. The cost of hoeing an acre of corn is 8 fish for Callie. Callie is the high-cost producer of corn hoeing, compared to Annie. Annie is the high-cost producer of fishing, compared to Callie. On average, every fish Annie catches requires the sacrifice of 0.20 acres of hoed corn (divide 4 acres by 20 fish per day). Every fish Callie catches requires the sacrifice of only 0.125 acres of hoed corn (divide 2 acres by 16 fish per day). Given their physical and mental capabilities, Annie can specialize in hoeing corn and then acquire fish by trading acres of hoed corn to Callie for Callie's fish. Callie can specialize in fishing and acquire hoed corn by trading fish to Annie for Annie's corn hoeing.

A favorite lesson of economists who teach a foundational class in economics is to demonstrate to their neophyte students that through specialization in production, coupled with voluntary exchange, both

Annie and Callie can enjoy more fish and more hoed corn, compared to independent, solitary production. For example, Annie, who is the low-cost producer of hoed corn, can hoe 3 acres of corn a day for herself and 1 acre a day for Callie. Callie, who is the low cost producer of fish, can fish all day and trade 6 of her 16 fish for 1 acre of corn hoeing, which Annie offers in exchange. Callie ends up with 1 acre of hoed corn per day and 10 fish per day. Annie ends up with 3 acres of hoed corn per day and 6 fish per day. If Annie and Callie produce both fish and hoed corn independently for themselves, without specialization and voluntary exchange, Annie could have 3 acres of hoed corn but only 5 fish per day, while Callie could have 1 acre of hoed corn but only 8 fish per day. Just as the classical economist David Ricardo taught us long ago, people are better off through specialization in production combined with voluntary exchange, compared to independent, solitary production of the goods and services they want.[107]

If the example of fish and hoed corn just above seems a bit technical and eye-glazing, do not despair. The example is not essential for understanding human willingness and ability to exchange value for value. Adam Smith also observed in *The Wealth of Nations* that people have a propensity to "truck, barter and exchange one thing for another."[108] Voluntary exchange—people willingly and freely choosing to trade one thing for another—is an unusually important kind of human interaction. Most of us exchange our labor services for goods and services produced by others, whether we are doctors, accountants, store clerks, teachers, or any of thousands of other vocations. Yes, we first exchange our labor for money, and then exchange our money for goods and services we want, but the money is just a medium of exchange. We don't really want the money we receive for our labor services. Money is only a temporary store of value that greatly facilitates voluntary exchange with others.

Through self-production alone, without voluntary exchange, none of us would be able to enjoy the wide range of goods and services we want. We would not know how to produce most goods and services for ourselves, even if we were so inclined. The celebrated article, *I, Pencil*, published in 1958 by Leonard E. Read, explains how no *one* person knows how or is able to make even something as simple as an ordinary #2 pencil.[109] Readers who have not already read *I, Pencil*, will find the article a fascinating and revealing insight into the power of voluntary exchange to generate human prosperity.

Each of us tends to specializes in producing goods or services for which we have a comparative advantage. We then exchange what we own from our own production to acquire nearly all other goods and services we want—goods and services produced by others. We don't know how to produce all those other goods; moreover, we would not want to, or be able to, even if we did know how. The resulting reduction in our wealth and value forgone (cost) due to solitary self-production would simply be too excessive. Specialization, division of labor, and voluntary exchange are the engines that enable the unparalleled success of capitalism in generating human prosperity.

As Aristotle said, humans are social and political animals. As social animals, people interact with others almost continuously. But all human interactions (many of which are exchanges—trading one thing for another) occur in one of just two possible modes: voluntary or compulsory. Voluntary exchanges are those that people choose freely without overt aggressive force, threat of force, or intentional deception from either party to the exchange. Compulsory exchanges are those forced upon us by another, either by overt aggressive force, threat of force, or intentional deception initiated by one of the parties to the exchange.

Aristotle in ancient Greece (384 BCE), and Pope Benedict the 16th in the 21st Century, both got it wrong, saying as they did that "just" exchange (trading) requires exchange of equal values. In fact, voluntary exchange creates greater value for both parties to the exchange. If it didn't, people wouldn't bother exchanging one thing for another. If Bobby offers Callie a dozen eggs in exchange for two fish, and Callie voluntarily agrees to the exchange, *both* Bobby and Callie have reason to say "thank you," because each receives greater value in return for the value given up. Why else would Bobby part with a dozen eggs? Why else would Callie give up two fish?

Tyro: What if I were dying of thirst in a desert. Along comes a water caravan, just in time to save me from dying. But the owner of the caravan tells me he sells water for $100 a gallon. Am I not compelled to pay his outrageous price to stay alive? I would not voluntarily exchange $100 for a gallon of water if I didn't have to. I would need the water to stay alive.

Solon: Who says you have to stay alive, Tyro? If you pay the vendor's price, you evidently agree that a gallon of water is more valuable to you than whatever else you could do with your $100.

Tyro: I certainly would want to stay alive. If I want to stay alive, I have to pay $100. That doesn't seem like voluntary exchange to me.

Solon: But voluntary it is. You get to choose among competing values without compulsion from the water vendor. You compare the value of spending your $100 one way—on a gallon of the vendor's water—to the value of spending the money in various different ways. If you buy the water, clearly you value the water more than myriad other ways you could spend your $100.

Tyro: I can die or I can pay $100 for water. I don't like my options.

Solon: Life is often like that, Tyro. Is the water vendor required for some reason to offer terms of trade that you like?

Tyro: Better terms of trade would be the right thing to do.

Solon: No, Tyro, better terms of trade might be a *good* thing to do—good for you, certainly, and perhaps even good for the vendor—good for the vendor's soul, perhaps. Aristotle, Plato, and other ancient philosophers believed that virtuous behavior is good for one's soul. But the water vendor has but one duty; to act morally. The vendor acts morally so long as he does not compel you. If

	both you and the vendor exchange voluntarily, both you and the vendor receive greater value than given up.
Tyro:	But wouldn't the vendor be compelling me to die if I do not pay $100 for water? Wouldn't that be immoral. What if I don't have $100 dollars?
Solon:	The vendor compels you in no way. The vendor broadens your opportunities; he does not diminish them. Compelling others always diminishes opportunities for others. If you do not have $100, perhaps the vendor would extend credit, if you asked. Perhaps the vendor would even give you water if you asked. Most people do behave virtuously, after all. Virtuous behavior is all around us most of the time.

Robert Nozick wrote in Anarchy, State, and Utopia,

> *A person's choice among differing degrees of unpalatable alternatives is not rendered nonvoluntary by the fact that others voluntarily chose and acted within their rights in a way that did not provide him with a more palatable alternative.*[110]

But as Robert Nozick wrote, "whether a person's actions are voluntary depends on what it is that limits his alternatives. If facts of nature do so (... or actions of others that are within their rights), the actions are voluntary."[111] Certainly, the actions of others may impose limits on our opportunities. But if the actions of others are moral, our choices among available alternatives are voluntary. Nozick illustrated the point with the fascinating example that follows:

> *Suppose there are twenty-six women and twenty-six men each wanting to be married. For each sex, all of that sex agree on the same ranking of the twenty-six members of the opposite sex*

> *in terms of desirability as marriage partners: call them A to Z and A' to Z' respectively in decreasing preferential order. A and A' voluntarily choose to get married, each preferring the other to any other partner. B would most prefer to marry A', and B' would most prefer to marry A, but by their choices A and A' have removed these options. When B and B' marry, their choices are not made nonvoluntary merely by the fact that there is something else they each would rather do. This other most preferred option requires the cooperation of others who have chosen, as is their right, not to cooperate. B and B' chose among fewer options than did A and A'. This contraction of the range of options continues down the line until we come to Z and Z', who each face a choice between marrying the other or remaining unmarried. Each prefers any one of the twenty-five other partners who by their choices have removed themselves from consideration by Z and Z'. Z and Z' voluntarily choose to marry each other. The fact that their only other alternative is (in their view) much worse, and the fact that others chose to exercise their rights in certain ways, thereby shaping the external environment of options in which Z and Z' choose, does not mean they did not marry voluntarily.*[112]

People act within their rights so long as they do not compel others unjustly. We may not like the actions of another person for many reasons, each of which reasons no doubt entails something we ourselves do not value. Our personal evaluations of another's actions may have bearing on whether that person's actions are virtuous, but not on whether the other person's actions are moral, so long as we are not compelled unjustly.

Voluntary exchange is the mechanism of Adam Smith's metaphor of the invisible hand. Smith wrote in *The Wealth of Nations* the oft quoted words,

> *It is not from the benevolence of the butcher the brewer, or the baker that we expect our dinner, but from their regard to their*

own interest. We address ourselves, not to their humanity, but to their self-love, and never talk to them of our own necessities, but of their advantages.[113]

Smith understood that voluntary exchange is motivated by each person seeking to gain additional value from the trade, with each party to a voluntary exchange knowing that he or she must offer value for value, else no exchange will occur.

Without voluntary exchange, social cooperation is unlikely, if not impossible. Voluntary exchange enhances individuals' awareness of others and their desires, including total strangers. In a society that insists that exchanges must be voluntary (a.k.a., a capitalistic society), one can't prosper without supplying some good or service that others want. Moreover, in a capitalist society that allows *only* voluntary exchange, people who best supply goods and services that others want will prosper most. People who produce little or nothing that others want are unlikely to prosper in a capitalist society, except by the benevolence of others.

Voluntary exchange relies on persuasion instead of force to accomplish human interaction. Persuasion or force are the only two modes of human interaction possible. If Bobby wants Annie's cabin, he can persuade Annie to trade with him, or he can force Annie to accept his chickens in trade for her cabin. No other possibilities exist. Capitalism relies on and requires persuasion; all other systems of political economy rely on force, in one way or another.

Tyro: Suppose I live in a small town with unusually limited job opportunities. Suppose the only work available is hard manual labor at a textile mill, and suppose the pay for such labor is really quite low—below what some people call a "living wage." Am I not compelled to work for the owner of the textile mill for whatever wage

	offered? That sort of job may be exchange, but it doesn't seem voluntary.
Solon:	Would the owner of the textile mill force you to work at the mill?
Tyro:	No, but I wouldn't have any other options.
Solon:	Could you choose to live and work elsewhere, somewhere that affords better job opportunities? Could you choose to start and operate your own business? Is it the mill owner's responsibility to provide alternatives you find attractive?
Tyro:	Isn't it immoral for the owner of the mill to offer such low wages, causing me to remain poor and live in poverty?
Solon:	The owner of the mill offers unforced employment, an opportunity for voluntary exchange, thereby *expanding* your opportunities. You choose to accept the terms offered or not. I see no compulsion, and therefore, no possibility of immorality on the part of the mill owner.
Tyro:	Well, having such poor alternatives doesn't seem fair.
Solon:	What do you mean by "fair," Tyro?
Tyro:	(after a prolonged silence) Fair means equal. Outcomes are fair if everyone ends up with the same access to goods and services.
Solon:	So, in Threesville, you think it would be fair if Annie, Bobby, and Callie share equally all the goods and services each produces, even though Annie produces six times as much as Callie and three times as much as Bobby each day, and even though Annie, Bobby, and Callie do not want the same goods and services, being individuals as they are, with entirely personal values, likes, and dislikes?
Tyro:	It isn't Callie's fault that she is not as able to produce goods and services as well as Annie and Bobby. Besides, everyone wants food, shelter, and other basic needs.
Solon:	If you must speak of fault, is it Annie's or Bobby's fault that Callie is less able? Does everyone want the same food, shelter, and whatever else you think are basic needs?

Tyro: No, of course not. But Callie is entitled to at least some minimal level of goods and services to meet her basic needs.

Solon: What are Callie's "minimal" basic needs, Tyro? And if Callie is "entitled," as you say, who has responsibility to provide Callie's entitlement to minimal basic needs, and why would Bobby or Annie have such responsibility?

Tyro: Callie's basic needs are enough food, shelter, and other stuff like health care to stay alive. Society has the responsibility to make sure everyone has enough to live a decent life.

Solon: Society does not exist, Tyro. Please speak of Bobby, Annie, and Callie in Threesville, not society. Do you now propose that "fair" means having just enough food, shelter, and "stuff" to stay alive?

Tyro: That's not what I mean.

Solon: What *do* you mean, Tyro? You seem to have moved away from the notion that "fair" means "equal," which is good, since equal outcomes for all is not possible, and hardly anyone thinks equal outcomes for all would be desirable, even if it were possible.

Tyro: I guess I don't really know how to say what "fair" means.

Solon: You are not alone, Tyro, even though people use the word as if it had a clear, definite meaning that is known to all. I prefer not use the word "fair," since I am unable to define the word.

Sometimes people are inclined to claim they have no choice, if the alternatives available are not to their liking. "I had to steal," says the thief. "I didn't have money to buy food for my family." Others are inclined to claim that it isn't fair that their lot in life is so materialistically meager. Stealing, some might say, is just "righting the wrong." This point of view is particularly common if theft is accomplished by elected officials (through mandatory taxation) for redistribution of income. Such notions of "fair" seem to undergird John Rawls's notion of "justice as fairness."[114]

Voluntary exchange is the second foundational, defining element of capitalism. Any system of political economy that compels exchange (e.g., slavery, drafting people into the army, or requiring people to buy health insurance) is not capitalism. Nor is a system of political economy that limits voluntary exchange (e.g., forbidding the sale of alcohol on Sunday, forbidding cutting hair commercially without a license, or forbidding people to give investment advice for a fee without approval of the state's bureaucracy).

Private property is the first defining element of capitalism. Voluntary exchange is the second, but second only because without private property, voluntary exchange is not possible. In the end, voluntary exchange is the very core of capitalism.

FREEDOM

Jean-Jacques Rousseau opened his treatise *The Social Contract* with the words, "man is born free, and everywhere he is in chains."[115] But people who live in a truly capitalist society are not in chains. Capitalism requires that people be free to act as they choose, provided their actions respect the Moral Imperative. Capitalism requires that people be free to choose all aspects of their lives without interference from others. Capitalism requires that people be free to choose where to live, what occupation to pursue, what kind of car to drive, who to associate with (and who not to associate with), who to contract with (and who not to contract with), and thousands of other choices. Capitalism requires freedom—freedom constrained only by the moral law.

Rousseau proposed that individuals should and would agree to sacrifice personal freedom in return for protection of their remaining rights, as did Thomas Hobbes, John Locke, and more recently, John Rawls. But what these four philosophers and many other proponents of social contract theory failed to grasp is that freedom is *inalienable* for rational beings, and that freedom is the natural, logical consequence of people obeying the Moral Imperative. Notwithstanding the theories of Hobbes, Locke, Rousseau, and Rawls, rational beings do not willingly abjure personal freedom, agreeing tacitly or explicitly to be compelled by state operatives. Whether the state operatives are monarchs, dictators, or legislatures elected by majority rule makes no difference whatsoever.

Rational people have but one right, the right to be free of unjust compulsion of others. Unjust compulsion is aggressive force, threat of force, or deception with intent to benefit the aggressor and disadvantage the person compelled. The only "social contract" that rational people agree to is "I will not compel you, if you will not compel me." Agreeing to allow another to compel us in return for "social order" is the antithesis of freedom and is a logical contradiction.

Freedom to choose one's actions, limited only by the Moral Imperative and just law is the third foundational, defining element of capitalism. Denial or restriction of personal freedom is antithetical to capitalism, whether the denial comes from a tyrant dictator or government operatives elected by a majority of voters. Throughout human history, some people have been more than willing to deny freedom to others. That propensity of a small minority of people, people who are willing to ignore and violate the Moral Imperative, gives rise to the fourth essential element of capitalism—just law.

LAW

> *Can the law—which necessarily requires the use of force—rationally be used for anything except protecting the rights of everyone? I defy anyone to extend it beyond this purpose without perverting it and, consequently, turning might against right.*
>
> CLAUDE FRÉDÉRIC BASTIAT[116]

What is law? Why do societies have laws? What is the purpose of law? Where do laws come from? Under what conditions is law authoritative? Philosophers, theologians, legal scholars, novelists, and playwrights have written copiously since antiquity to offer answers to these questions. This brief essay on law seeks only to explain how *just law* is the fourth defining and essential element of capitalism.

Law is a set of explicit, codified rules that all members of a society are obliged to obey. Through the institutions of government, law is promulgated, interpreted, and enforced by government operatives (elected or appointed), with explicit penalties for violation of the law.

All societies adopt laws. Members of a society adopt laws to guide, prescribe and proscribe behavior for members of society, which is the purpose of law. Thomas Hobbes believed that a powerful, compelling state—a leviathan—was necessary to keep people from compelling one another, or as Hobbes put it, an all-powerful state to "over-awe them all."[117]

Throughout human history, some people have been willing and able to violate the Moral Imperative. Consequently, law and enforcement of law by force seem to be necessary for humans to live together in society. Hobbes placed his confidence in an all-powerful state to make and enforce laws. Kant, on the other hand, believed that *just law* must ultimately come from within us, which leads us to ideas about the source and authority of law.

All law is one of two kinds: natural law or positive law. Natural law comprises inherent inalienable rights of people, conferred not by acts of legislation or dictate, but by God, human nature, or reason (depending on one's beliefs about deity). Positive law (from the infinitive "to posit") is law stipulated by particular persons (such as a legislature or a king or a dictator) that specifies and requires specific action. Positive law applies at a certain time and place (not universally). Positive law is statutory law, created by government operatives of an organized society.

Natural law is authorized entirely by human reason and logic. As Thomas Aquinas explained in the Prima Secundae of the *Summa Theologica*, natural law springs from practical rationality of humans (which rationality Aquinas believed came from God). Natural law is universally binding for humans and universally knowable by humans.[118] Natural law is *just law*, because it stipulates equal rights for all people.

But the only right that all people can have equally, without violating the same right of others, is to be free of compulsion from others. In the end, natural law is the Moral Imperative.

Paradoxically, positive law claims to be self-authorizing. The source of all positive law is some particular person or set of persons, who are authorized *by law* to create laws! According to positive law theory, we are obliged to obey positive law *because it is the law*. Positive law is a curious kind of self-licking ice cream cone. The authorization for positive law is positive law.

Writing in *The Market for Liberty*,[119] Morris and Linda Tannehill object to any statutory law whatsoever. They argue that all one has to do is ask if one is aggressing against another to decide if an act is justly legal. But members of society may benefit from some positive law, e.g., drive on the right-hand side of the road, contracts for sale of real estate must be in writing, the age of majority is 18 for voting, and so on. Some positive laws merely coordinate certain actions of members of society and are beneficial or neutral for nearly all members of a society. The kind of positive law the Tannehills and other classical liberal philosophers reject is law that benefits one set of people at the expense of another.

Bastiat put the matter this way:

> *But how is this legal plunder to be identified? Quite simply. See if the law takes from some persons what belongs to them, and gives it to other persons to whom it does not belong. See if the law benefits one citizen at the expense of another by doing what the citizen himself cannot do without committing a crime.*[120]

Bastiat's essay, *The Law*, is a classic statement of the distinction between *just law* and *unjust law*. In that essay he writes,

> *What is law? What ought it to be? What is its scope; its limits? Logically, at what point do the just powers of the legislator stop?*

I do not hesitate to answer: Law is the common force organized to act as an obstacle to injustice. In short, law is justice.[121]

The law is the organization of the natural right of lawful defense. It is the substitution of a common force for individual forces. And this common force is to do only what the individual forces have a natural and lawful right to do: to protect persons, liberties, and properties; to maintain the right of each, and to cause justice to reign over us all.[122]

When law and force keep a person within the bounds of justice, they impose nothing but a mere negation. They oblige him only to abstain from harming others.[123]

But when the law, by means of its necessary agent, force, imposes upon men a regulation of labor, a method or a subject of education, a religious faith or creed – then the law is no longer negative; it acts positively upon people. It substitutes the will of the legislator for their own wills; the initiative of the legislator for their own initiatives. When this happens, the people no longer need to discuss, to compare, to plan ahead; the law does all this for them. Intelligence becomes a useless prop for the people; they cease to be men; they lose their personality, their liberty, their property.[124]

A substantial portion of positive law in the world today is plunder. Positive law that goes beyond the beneficial coordination of social interaction (e.g., stop at red lights) is immoral, if it imposes by force the will of one set of people on another.

Capitalism is a social system of political economy defined by these four essential elements: private property, voluntary exchange, freedom, and just law. Any social system of political economy that lacks these elements is not capitalism, and should not be called capitalism, if clarity and meaning of expression are valued.

IS CAPITALISM MORAL?

If morality is respect for and self-willed obedience to the Moral Imperative, and if capitalism is a social system of political economy that consistently requires private property, voluntary exchange, freedom, and just law, then capitalism is moral; moreover, capitalism is the only system of political economy that is moral. A straightforward syllogism makes the case:

Major Premise: Compelling people unjustly is immoral.
Minor Premise: Capitalism does not compel people unjustly.
Conclusion: Capitalism is moral.

Any system of political economy that includes or allows unjust compulsion of one by another—or compulsion of one set of people (members of society) by another set of people (government operatives)—is immoral, by the same logic. Socialism, communism, democratic socialism, fascism, monarchy, and every other system of political economy aside from capitalism, not only allow, but *require* for their very existence, unjust compulsion of one by another. Consequently, not only is capitalism moral, it is the only system of political economy that is moral.

7

What Capitalism Is Not

To condemn free-market capitalism because of anything going on today makes no sense. There is no evidence that capitalism exists today.

RON PAUL[125]

WHY IS CAPITALISM SO REVILED?

History shows unequivocally that the four principles of capitalism work to generate widespread prosperity for humans, whenever and wherever they are practiced together consistently. That conclusion is no longer much debated, because the historical evidence is so clear and unambiguous.[126,127] Private property, voluntary exchange, freedom, and just law obviously "work" to generate widespread prosperity for humans. Yet, for all its success in generating human material prosperity, capitalism is reviled by hundreds of millions of people around the globe. Googling the phrase "capitalism images," yields anecdotal evidence of just how reviled capitalism is. The Google search produces a panoply of images that convey negative, evil, or diabolical meanings for capitalism, with scarcely a positive, good, or inspiring image to be found. Why? Why is capitalism so denigrated? Why do so many people believe that capitalism is immoral?

Tyro: Solon, why *does* capitalism have such a bad name? Even the most cursory review of human history shows that societies that come closest to practicing the principles of capitalism are the most prosperous and afford the greatest freedom to citizens of the society.

Solon: Perhaps many people do not know what capitalism really is and what it really is not. Perhaps many people believe capitalism is something it is not.

[handwritten margin note: can't you say this about other systems?]

To better understand why so many people despise capitalism, we must understand what capitalism really is *not*, yet is so often mistaken to be. Envision a continuum with two polar cases. On the right end of the continuum is capitalism. In a society that practiced capitalism, most land would be privately owned; human interaction would be entirely voluntary; people would be free to choose all aspects of their lives, free of unjust compulsion from others; nearly all law would be natural law, with very little positive law. Such positive law as existed would be arbitrary rules to enable social coordination; e.g., drive on the right-hand side of the road; green means "go," red means "stop," or rules that codify social agreements reached by *near-unanimous* agreement; e.g., the age of sexual majority is 18; or, contracts with minors are unenforceable.

On the left end of the continuum, to give it a name, is tyranny—the opposite of capitalism. The opposite of capitalism would be a system of political economy that features little or no privately owned land; human interaction would be highly proscribed, restricted, and regulated by force of the state; most aspects of people's lives would be dictated by compulsion (you *will* comply, as with *Star Trek's* Borg); most laws would be positive law, most of which would vitiate and nullify natural law. In the lived world of some 185 countries, we find no societies at either polar case of the continuum, of course. What we find is countries closer to either the left or right poles of the continuum.

Countries closer to the pole of capitalism include Hong Kong, Singapore, Australia, New Zealand, Switzerland, Canada, Denmark, and the United States. Most countries lie somewhere in the mid-range of the continuum. Countries closer to the pole of tyranny include North Korea, Cuba, Zimbabwe, Venezuela, Eritrea, Burma, Democratic Republic of Congo, Equatorial Guinea, Turkmenistan, and Iran.[128] Readers can make their own lists, of course.

No one mistakes the tyranny of despotic regimes or military regimes for capitalism. No one is confused or puzzled about whether Cuba, North Korea, Egypt, Russia, Venezuela, or Iran are capitalist societies. Clearly, they are not. But what about America, Canada, England, Japan, and Germany? Are these countries capitalist societies? Put simply—not really. For even in the political economies of these countries, we find disregard for private property (e.g., in America, Kelo vs. New London, CT; federal government ownership of vast tracts of land in the western states), blatant restrictions on voluntary exchange (e.g., so-called blue laws in America, England, and Canada), inexplicable limitations of personal freedom (e.g., licensing requirements for cutting hair commercially, of all things), and ever-growing volumes of plunderous positive law. Although America and a few other countries are *called* capitalist countries—by friends and foes alike—they really are quite far from true capitalism.

The United States of America is the poster child of capitalism, is it not? If we find widespread characteristics of the political economy in America that are immoral and loathsome, surely we should condemn capitalism, shouldn't we? The "occupy-Wall-Street" crowd lambastes Wall Street and its "lions of finance," cursing them as capitalists and calling their actions capitalism. The "give-peace-a-chance" crowd points to the military-industrial complex in America, cursing large corporations in the defense industry as capitalists and calling their actions capitalism. The "health-care-is-a-fundamental-right" crowd points to the health-care industrial complex in America, cursing its insurance corporations and big pharma corporations (a.k.a., "corporatism"), calling their actions capitalism.

But Wall Street, the recipient of stupefying federal bailouts and government favoritism, is certainly *not* capitalism. The military-industrial complex in America, with its recurring cycle of massive, federally financed production of large-scale weapons, Presidents (with the acquiescence of Congress) making war with countries that pose no serious threat to America, followed by more federal purchase of more, evermore sophisticated weapons, is *not* capitalism. The healthcare-industrial complex in America, with its closely guarded barriers to entry, price controls, and subsidies also is *not* capitalism. A much more apt and descriptive name for the political economy practiced in America and other countries that are commonly called capitalist would be "democratic cronyism," not capitalism. Such a political economy is democratic, because we all get to vote; it is cronyism because ... well, it *is* cronyism.

 Typically, people who rail so passionately against capitalism—calling it immoral and despicable—are really railing against democratic cronyism. As Solon suggests, perhaps the foes of capitalism really do not know what capitalism is—what it really is—and what it really is not.

Are there elements of other systems we miss/ignore b/c we are looking at it as 1 big bad thing

DEMOCRATIC CRONYISM

Democratic cronyism is a system of political economy that includes some or all of the following:

- Regular elections of government operatives (a.k.a., politicians) who are usually elected by simple majority, but candidates who get on the ballot for elections is closely controlled by government operatives; who gets to vote for which candidates is also closely controlled by government operatives;
- Malleable laws, which can change with the pronouncements of top government operatives, even if a constitution is enshrined as the supreme law of the land (as it is in practically every country on earth); the constitution is said to be "interpreted" by courts (whose judges are often appointed by other government operatives) to be a "living" constitution, with no enduring principles that cannot be ignored;

- Favoritism and privilege granted by government operatives to particular persons, businesses, or industries; concentrated benefits to the few with costs widely distributed across tax payers as the general rule;
- Subsidies granted by government operatives (often through the tax code) that favor particular persons, businesses, or industries over others; again, concentrated benefits to the few with costs widely distributed across tax payers as the general rule;
- Tax advantages, loop holes, or so-called "tax preferences" (if you like the obfuscation of economic jargon) that favor one individual, business, or industry over others; again, concentrated benefits to the few with costs widely distributed across tax payers as the general rule;
- Legal barriers to entry into industries or professional activities (in the form of positive laws), often in the form of licensing required from a government agency (e.g., SEC, FCC, FTC, FERC, etc.), or perhaps licensing from an appointed "institutional authority" that is purported to be a "non-governmental organization" (e.g., FINRA, FDIC, ABA, AMA, etc.);
- Trade associations and labor unions financed by mandatory fees for membership, which use the mandatory fees to lobby government operatives and to provide financial support for particular political candidates who support the associations' and the unions' special interests (think K Street in the United States);
- Legal prosecution of certain individuals or businesses for infringement of certain government regulations, with a blind eye afforded other individuals or businesses who also violate the same regulations (recall Martha Stewart?);
- A stupefying preponderance of rules and regulations written in copious, ambiguous, eye-glazing legalese by bureaucrats (employees of elected government operatives), which allows bureaucrats and courts to apply rules and regulations unevenly and capriciously;
- Bailouts, financed by tax dollars, for businesses said by government operatives to be "too big to fail"; again, concentrated benefits to the few with costs widely distributed across tax payers as the general rule;

- Money creation by a central bank (the Fed in the United States) that directly finances government spending (60% of which spending is transfer payments from Annie to Callie) or props up businesses and whole industries that have friends in high governmental places;
- Loans guaranteed by the government (which reduces the cost of borrowing) for particular businesses or industries, but which are available *only* to particular persons, businesses, or industries;
- Protection of domestic businesses from international competitors, via tariffs and non-tariff trade restrictions; certain businesses and industries benefit, but hundreds of millions of consumers pay prices higher than would prevail without trade restrictions (consider, for example, sugar and other "essential" commodities like mohair in the United States);
- No-bid contracts for tax-financed expenditures offered by government operatives to particular persons or businesses operating in particular industries (a.k.a. formerly called earmarks in the United States).

If the all-too familiar practices listed above describe the system of political economy in which you live, you can be certain that you do not live in a capitalist society. People who call such systems of political economy "capitalism," would more aptly call them by a more descriptive, more accurate name—democratic cronyism.

Some critics indict capitalism for the reprehensible practices of democratic cronyism by arguing that capitalism *causes* cronyism.[129] These critics argue that in a capitalist society, some individuals earn large incomes. Large incomes lead to great wealth. Great wealth leads to political power—which is to say, influence over the apparatus of government—which alone has the authority to compel others legally with force. Influence with the institutions of government inevitably leads to cronyism, such critics say, since wealthy people use their influence with government operatives to benefit themselves. Hence, the critics conclude, capitalism *is* cronyism.

These same critics turn a blind eye to the blatant cronyism practiced in countries like North Korea, China, Iran, Zimbabwe, Iraq, Saudi Arabia, Venezuela, Mexico, and nearly all the countries of Africa—countries that no one mistakes for capitalist countries. Capitalism is not cronyism, and as an observable empirical fact, cronyism is most present and damaging in countries that explicitly abjure the principles of capitalism.

How strange, that so many opponents of capitalism point to the cronyism that pervades the American political economy (which it does), but are evidently blind to the cronyism of other countries that are expressly not capitalistic. Cronyism rightfully deserves severe criticism and rejection by all people who wish to behave morally and who want to live in a society that insists on moral behavior. Democratic cronyism is immoral, requiring as it does, unjust compulsion exercised through the power of government operatives. Other systems of political economy other than capitalism are also immoral, including democratic socialism (and other flavors of socialism), fascism, dictatorship, military regime. All systems of political economy other than capitalism require unjust compulsion exercised through the power of government; they simply cannot function without it.

Democratic cronyism is *not* capitalism. Cronyism is cronyism, democratic or not, wherever and whenever it is practiced, which sadly enough, is just about everywhere on the planet throughout all of human history, as Hunter Lewis has documented in *Cronyism in America*.[130] As Ayn Rand[131] and Ludwig von Mises[132] wrote, capitalism is an "unknown ideal." But cronyism is as common as rain. It seems that what many self-proclaimed critics of capitalism *truly* revile is cronyism, not capitalism, but the critics have conflated these two very different systems of political economy.

The oxymora "crony capitalism," and "state capitalism" are terms that subtly promote the incorrect conflation of cronyism and capitalism. The notion of so-called "mixed economies," a term popularized by just about every principles of economics textbook published in the last 50 years, further obfuscates the clear distinctions between cronyism, statism, and true capitalism. Mixed economies, say the textbooks, are a "blend" of free market capitalism with command and control policies administered by the state (for the "common good," it is said). But such blandishment is like conceiving of a blend of fire and ice, a blend of life and death, a blend of silence and sound, a blend of force and freedom. One annihilates the other.

Any number of writers have prefaced the word "capitalism" with one or another adjective. In addition to crony capitalism and state capitalism, we have the following impressive array: anarcho-capitalism, welfare capitalism, predatory capitalism, laissez-faire capitalism, Rhine capitalism, corporate capitalism, monopoly capitalism, techno-capitalism, and disaster capitalism. But the adjectives obfuscate, rather than clarify, for they all convey something about capitalism that capitalism really is not.

—☙—

Tyro: Solon, some of my teachers tell us that capitalism is unjust, runs on greed, creates economic inequality, exploits the masses, and destroys the environment. What about those claims? Are my teachers wrong?

Solon: Perhaps your teachers have not noticed the massively greater injustice, greed, inequality, exploitation, and disregard for the environment that is engendered by all systems of political economy *other* than capitalism. It is more than just a happy coincidence that capitalism is both moral *and* generates wide-spread prosperity. Indeed, what a strange, unfathomable world it would be, if the only system of political economy that in fact does generate human prosperity were immoral.

Your teachers cannot define "unjust," aside from what we all agree is immoral. Your teachers cannot define "greed" in a way that does not include everyone. Your teachers cannot explain how economic equality can be even attempted—never mind achieved—without using force to compel others unjustly, for free people will not be economically equal, and economically equal people will not be free. Your teachers cannot find exploited masses anywhere in the lived world, except in countries that deny explicitly the principles of capitalism. Your teachers somehow miss the observable, empirical fact that the environment is most damaged and disregarded in countries like China, which disavow the principles of capitalism.

Are your teachers wrong, Tyro? I will ask you to answer your own question.

8

Morality, Capitalism, and the Good Society

Capitalism is relatively new in human history. Prior to capitalism, the way people amassed great wealth was by looting, plundering, and enslaving their fellow man. Capitalism made it possible to become wealthy by serving your fellow man.

WALTER WILLIAMS[133]

THE GOOD SOCIETY

What is the good society? In the *Republic,* Plato wrote about the idea of justice and what he thought would comprise the good society, for surely, whatever else it is, the good society must be just. In this most famous of Plato's dialogues, Socrates proposes that, "we enquire into the nature of justice and injustice, first as they appear in the State, and secondly in the individual, proceeding from the greater to the lesser and comparing them."[134] Socrates thinks that seeing what justice is at the level of society and the state will be easier; he also thinks that justice and injustice will have the same meaning for the individual as the state.

But Socrates got it backwards. Society is not an existent, nor is the state the representative of society. Society is nothing more than the collection of individuals who comprise it. The state is nothing more than a small set of individuals who claim the right to compel everyone else with force and threat of force—as official representatives of society. Society does not act; only individuals act, although they often do so in a social context. Society does not choose just acts or unjust acts; only individuals do. Consequently, if society (or the state) will be just and good, that result will obtain, if and only if, the individuals who comprise society are just and good. If we want to understand what justice is, we must look for it in the actions and interactions of individuals.

In the *Republic*, Plato argues through the words of Socrates that justice in the state is "keeping one's place" (to use the words of Karl Popper).[135] For Plato, keeping one's place in a well-ordered, and hence, just and good society, was as a member of one of three classes: soldiers, producers, or rulers. Each class had a preordained role to play. If the rulers would create laws (the philosopher-kings), and if soldiers (the eugenically bred guardians) would enforce the laws, and if producers would obey authority and get the work done, then a society would be "just," according to Plato and Socrates.

Socrates then moves to justice for individuals. Justice in individuals, he argues, is the supreme virtue, comprising the other three cardinal human virtues of temperance, wisdom, and courage—all in proper balance, comparable to the balance of guardians, producers, and kings in the just and good society, as Plato and Socrates see it.

Plato's *Republic* offers a vision of the just and good society that very few people find satisfying, agreeable, or even remotely sensible. Plato tells us that the just and good society is like a colony of termites, of all things! As it happens, every termite in a colony belongs to one of three distinct castes: soldier, worker, or reproducer. Each colony has but one king and one queen (the reproducers). Interestingly enough, only the king and queen have eyes and can "see" (like Plato's philosopher-king who emerges from the cave of projected images and is able to see "true" reality); the other termite castes are blind. Soldier termites, with their oversized mandibles, defend the colony against insect predators. Workers do all the work, creating the termitaria, foraging, creating food by digesting cellulose from wood, storing food, feeding the other castes, and maintaining the nest. For termites, the colony—not the individual termite—is the only thing that matters, with each member of the colony confined entirely to a distinct role, its "just" position in the colony. Of course, Plato probably didn't know he was describing a colony of termites when he proposed the nature of what he took to be a just and good society for humans, but the analogy is striking.

Like society, "the good" is also not an existent, even though literature around the world is full of the notion of good and evil as perennial foes. As Solon leads Tyro to understand, for a thing to be good, it must be good for something. The something that society can be good for is fostering, promoting, and engendering *cooperation* among its members, so that the members of a society may reap the enormous benefits of human cooperation. In his account of the pin factory, Adam Smith gave us in *Wealth of Nations* a clear and convincing statement of the power of human cooperation for producing material goods.[136] Ludwig von Mises elaborated in *Theory and History*, pointing out that cooperation to achieve desired ends is not only powerful, but almost without exception a human characteristic, a characteristic not usually seen in other forms of life.[137] Without doubt, the just and good society is a society that engenders cooperation among its members. Mises wrote,

> *The ultimate yardstick of justice is conduciveness to the preservation of social cooperation. Conduct suited to preserve social cooperation is just, conduct detrimental to the preservation of society is unjust. There cannot be any question of organizing society according to the postulates of an arbitrary preconceived idea of justice. The problem is to organize society for the best possible realization of those ends which men want to attain by social cooperation. Social utility is the only standard of justice.*[138]

Mises thought there could be no other standard or meaning for the idea of justice than social utility. He argued that ends chosen by humans are inexplicable, subjective, and based on individual values. "Means," according to Mises, must be evaluated only in terms of their ability to produce desired "ends." But Mises may not have seen that "means" that require compulsion of one person by another are themselves part of whatever else are "ends." If Bobby resorts to force, threat of force, or guile to compel Annie to achieve his desired end (even if Bobby claims and genuinely believes the end he desires is for the good of Callie), compulsion of Annie is *part of the ends*, not merely an independent means of achieving Bobby's inexplicable, subjectively desired ends. For all his brilliance in understanding the nature of human action and explaining the power of human cooperation, Mises may not have seen that the Moral Imperative is the very foundation of the idea of justice, without which, voluntary cooperation among humans is impossible.

The good society must be just and good for *all* its members at once. Taking property by force from Annie and giving it to Callie may seem just (to John Rawls[139] and his apologists), but how could compelling Annie with force, threat of force, or guile be just *also for Annie*? If Callie is in need—starving, let's say—then giving Callie food would certainly be virtuous. If Bobby or Annie or both agree voluntarily to give Callie food, then Threesville could be called a virtuous society, comprised as it would be of virtuous members. But if Bobby forces Annie against her will to give Callie food, justice is lost, because we no longer have justice for all. Again, moral behavior is a necessary condition for virtuous behavior. It's not clear how a society can be called just and good, if its members (or its governors, regardless of how they became governors) rely on force, threat of force, or guile to achieve desired ends, notwithstanding how desirable those ends may otherwise be.

LIFE WITHOUT CAPITALISM

We know what life without capitalism is like, for nearly all human history is the story of life without capitalism—life without secure private property, life with circumscribed and restricted voluntary exchange (restricted by compulsion), life without freedom, and life with a multitude of positive laws that oppose and vitiate just law. Humans existed for thousands of years in political economies that were nearly devoid of the four foundational principles of capitalism. We know that human existence throughout most of human history was squalid for all but a small number of aristocrats, whose higher quality of life depended entirely on force, threat of force, and guile.

In a presentation titled *The Greatest Story Ever Told*, Steven Landsburg tells the fascinating history of the evolution of human prosperity.[140]

> *Modern humans first emerged about 100,000 year ago. For the next 99,800 years or so, nothing happened. Well, not quite nothing. There were wars, political intrigue, the invention of agriculture—but none of that stuff had much effect on the quality of people's lives. Almost everyone lived on the modern equivalent of $400 to $600 a year, just above the subsistence level. True, there were always tiny aristocracies who lived far better, but numerically they were quite insignificant.*
>
> *Then—just a couple of hundred years ago, maybe 10 generations—people started getting richer. And richer and richer still. Per capita income, at least in the West, began to grow at the unprecedented rate of about three quarters of a percent per year. A couple of decades later, the same thing was happening around the world.*
>
> *Then, it got even better. By the 20th century, per capita real incomes, that is, incomes adjusted for inflation, were growing at 1.5% per year, on average, and for the past half century, they've been growing at about 2.3%. If you're earning a modest middle-class income of $50,000 a year, and if you expect your children, 25 years from now, to occupy that same modest rung on the economic ladder, then with a 2.3% growth rate, they'll be earning the inflation-adjusted equivalent of $89,000 a year. Their children, another 25 years down the line, will earn $158,000 a year.*[141]

What was it that happened a couple of hundred years ago that permitted the enormous and ever-growing increase in human well-being? Landsburg tells us that the source of this surge of wealth—the "engine of prosperity," as he puts it—is technological progress. He is right, of course. But that answer is quite incomplete, as Landsburg further explains, going on to say that the engine of technological progress is *ideas*. But ideas do not flourish and grow without a nourishing and encouraging political economy that fosters social cooperation. The history of humans shows that fact without doubt.

At about the same time that average income began its spectacular rise some 250 years ago, the world also saw the emergence of political economies in the West that permitted wide-spread and secure private property, a dramatic increase in less restricted voluntary exchange, a much larger measure of personal freedom and liberty than ever before, and emerging reliance on just law—instead of rule by kings and generals. Foremost of these political economies was a young America. For about 150 years in America, the four principles of capitalism had free expression. The resulting rise in prosperity was nothing short of spectacular. Yet, inexplicably, over the most recent 100 years, America has retreated from the principles of capitalism. We do so at our own peril.

Life without capitalism is life controlled by force, threat of force, and guile exercised by a small set of people called "government." As P.J. Proudhon wrote, [handwritten: does it make a difference if thats what ppl want? Monarchy--]

> *To be GOVERNED is to be watched, inspected, spied upon, directed, law-driven, numbered, regulated, enrolled, indoctrinated, preached at, controlled, checked, estimated, valued, censured, commanded, by creatures who have neither the right nor the wisdom nor the virtue to do so. To be GOVERNED is to be at every operation, at every transaction noted, registered, counted, taxed, stamped, measured, numbered, assessed, licensed, authorized, admonished, prevented, forbidden, reformed, corrected, punished. It is, under pretext of public utility, and in the name of the*

> *general interest, to be placed under contribution, drilled, fleeced, exploited, monopolized, extorted from, squeezed, hoaxed, robbed; then, at the slightest resistance, the first word of complaint, to be repressed, fined, vilified, harassed, hunted down, abused, clubbed, disarmed, bound, choked, imprisoned, judged, condemned, shot, deported, sacrificed, sold, betrayed; and to crown all, mocked, ridiculed, derided, outraged, dishonored. That is government; that is its justice; that is its morality.*[142]

What are the implicit beliefs of people who argue for life without capitalism? The opponents of capitalism—those who favor socialism, those who favor the welfare state, or some other form of statism—must believe that most people are immoral. They must believe that a few people know what is moral, but most people do not. They must believe that most people are stupid (a proposition founded on their own abundant arrogance). They must believe that some people are angelic, wise, and not self-interested (the ones who should be in charge, of course). They must believe that people can and should be forced to do what a small set of others want them to do (in the name of the "common good," of course). They must believe that compulsion of the many by the few is acceptable and necessary for humans; that individuals do not deserve in return for their services the services that others are willing to exchange *voluntarily*. They must believe that most people have no concern for others (therefore, people must be *forced* to behave charitably to support the poor). They must believe that most people are looters and free loaders who will be free-riders, if not compelled to pay compulsory taxes to finance what they, the government operatives, take to be the legitimate services of government.

Critics of capitalism—people who call for life without capitalism—evidently hold a dour, pessimistic view of their fellow citizens. They also hold an arrogant, self-serving view of their own perspicacity, and they are willing to bully others to insist on life without capitalism. Given the unequivocally miserable history of life without capitalism, the opponents of capitalism are also people with little regard for the welfare of other people, although they proclaim loudly and incessantly just the opposite.

Socialists, and all other "ists" who call for a leviathan state, are first and foremost egotists. They believe that some small set of humans (among whom they nearly always include themselves) knows what to produce, how to produce it, and for whom it should be produced. These "ists" pretend not to know, or they deny, that their schemes for social organization will *definitely* require compulsion of one human by another, which is to say, their schemes will require immoral behavior.

LIFE WITH CAPITALISM

Can we imagine life with true capitalism? Let us try. Unlike Plato, who thought we could better see justice and the good society by looking at the state, let us instead look to the citizens of Threesville, living together in a society whose smallness enables great clarity.

In a truly capitalistic Threesville, all but a trivial amount of land would be owned privately by Annie, Bobby, or Callie. Each would have acquired original ownership of land by homesteading. Subsequent transfer of land would occur entirely by voluntary exchange. A small amount of *unowned* land would comprise roads, a small "commons" (for the practical purposes of political interaction), and land that none of the three inhabitants of Threesville wanted to homestead—land which would remain available for homesteading, should other people arrive and wish to live in Threesville. Such unowned land would not be said to be owned by the state or "by the people." Of course, certain kinds of land in Threesville—the atmosphere, oceans, and rivers—would always remain unowned; none of the inhabitants of Threesville could homestead such land. Use and disposition of all such *unownable* land would necessarily have to be decided in a social context through the political institutions of Threesville.

In a capitalistic Threesville, *all* interaction among Annie, Bobby, and Callie would be voluntary, insofar as their interactions were in accord with just law. If we think about it, most human interaction is exchange of one thing for another. We are hard pressed to adduce examples of human interaction that are not exchange. As noted before, all human interaction is either *voluntary* or it is *compelled* by force, threat of force, or guile. In a capitalistic Threesville, compulsion of one by another would be strictly illegal, made so by natural law, which is founded on the Moral Imperative. All law in Threesville would be *just law*—which is to say a combination of natural law and small body of positive law adopted *unanimously* by Annie, Bobby, and Callie.

Threesville would have very few laws, and the few laws it did have would have been adopted unanimously. For in Threesville, it is obvious that Annie and Bobby have no more right to compel Callie, just because they voted as a majority to do so, than Annie has a right to compel Callie, or Bobby has a right to compel Annie, or Annie has a right to compel Bobby. As professor Bernardo de la Paz asks Wyoh in Robert Heinlein's *The Moon Is a Harsh Mistress*, "under what circumstances is it moral for a group to do that which is not moral for a member of the group to do alone"?[143] Do two people have the right to do to another what everyone agrees one person has no right to do to another? The answer to the Professor's question is obvious. There are no such circumstances.

The political institution of voting (i.e., democracy) would be the first and foremost political institution of a capitalistic Threesville, but the idea of "rule by majority" would hold no sway whatsoever. If a proposed law cannot be agreed to unanimously, it would *not* become law in Threesville.

Tyro: If laws must be passed unanimously, I don't think many laws could be passed.

Solon: Indeed, Tyro. That is the very point of requiring unanimity or near unanimity for codified positive law. Only *just* laws will be passed if unanimity is required.

The wide-spread political institution of majority rule is a principal cause of the ultimate decline of democratic societies, devolving as they do to democratic cronyism. We may recall that Plato despised democracy, believing that democracy devolves ultimately to tyranny—first the tyranny of the majority, followed by tyranny concentrated in the hand of a single tyrant. Inexplicably, something in many people seems to yearn for a king. Yet, Plato failed to see the real problem with democracy, which is not democracy itself (voting), but the political institution of majority rule. Democracy that requires unanimity or near unanimity for social decisions is the only political institution that is moral, because democracy that includes the political institution of majority rule ultimately devolves to the use of force, threat of force, or guile in the form of the all powerful state.

Threesville would have a government. Even a micro-society like Threesville will benefit from executive administration to attend to the legitimate, moral and beneficial services of government. But the government of a capitalistic Threesville would be *bound* first and always by natural law, and by whatever small set of positive laws Annie, Bobby, and Callie agreed unanimously to enforce; natural law and positive law adopted unanimously together *define* just law.

Suppose that Annie, Bobby and Callie vote to elect Annie to a term as President of Threesville. Majority rule would be allowed for electing government operatives, because unanimity might be impossible, and because in a capitalistic Threesville, government operatives are strictly bound by just law, which means that not much is riding on who exactly becomes a government operative. As President, Annie would have no power to do anything other than enforce the just laws of Threesville. The government of a capitalistic Threesville would be the "night watchman" government described and justified by Robert Nozick, which is the only moral government possible.[144]

None of the laws in Threesville would empower anyone to compel one or two of the others to do anything whatsoever. Strange as it might sound to citizens living in America (or living in any number of other political economies around the world that also are not capitalistic, but are thought to be), it is unlikely that Threesville would adopt laws that prohibited use of marijuana, cocaine, heroin, or any other drugs (which is not to propose that use of such drugs is a good thing). It is also unlikely that the laws of Threesville would prohibit prostitution or prohibit selling alcohol on Sunday or prohibit any other such actions that are sometimes called "victimless crimes"). Of course, Annie, Bobby, and Callie *could* adopt whatever positive laws they choose by unanimous agreement, so long as those laws did not violate the Moral Imperative, but not otherwise.

To sum up, in a capitalistic Threesville, the state would not be empowered to compel anyone unjustly. All interactions among Annie, Bobby, and Callie would be entirely voluntary. If Annie wanted Bobby to help her build a house, Bobby would have to agree, else it would not happen. If Bobby wanted Callie to produce corn and give it to Annie, Callie would have to agree, else it would not happen. If Callie wanted to produce eggs instead of corn, that would be *entirely* up to Callie. If Bobby preferred not to trade with Annie, that choice would belong to Bobby. In a capitalistic Threesville, Annie, Bobby, and Callie would be free to chose their actions without interference of one by another, limited only by just law.

Tyro: I can see that unanimity for passing positive laws is possible and necessary in a capitalistic Threesville, Solon, but what about in a society like ours that includes millions of people?

Solon: The high bar of unanimity for voting is infeasible in a large society, Tyro. Indeed, in most societies, true democracy (voting by all citizens directly) is infeasible, although technology may someday make it feasible. Representative government is all that is practical in societies much larger than a few hundred citizens. But majority rule is far too low a bar for adoption of positive law. The history of all political economies based on democratic majority rule shows that given sufficient time, democratic majority rule produces an abundance of positive laws that are immoral—laws that codify plunderous, unjust compulsion of the many by the few.

Tyro: If unanimity is not feasible, and majority rule leads to immoral positive law, what political institution can take its place?

Solon: Once the principle of unanimity is relaxed, the next stopping point becomes indeterminate, but not entirely arbitrary. As a practical matter, requiring a three-fourths majority, or better still, a four-fifths majority appears to be sufficient in most cases to prevent adoption of positive laws that vitiate natural law.

In a capitalistic Threesville, taxes would be paid, but they would be paid voluntarily. The government of Threesville would have no power to compel payment of taxes. Some people (critics of capitalism—of whom many are advocates of the leviathan welfare state) argue that the "free-rider problem" makes compulsory taxation necessary. According to the free-rider problem, most people will not pay for services of government, if they are not compelled to do so by mandatory taxes. Such critics have no historical evidence to support that claim. But even if evidence of that claim did exist, it wouldn't justify compulsory taxation. Compulsory taxation is immoral, since it is stealing. In Threesville, the influence of social ostracism from Callie and Bobby, should Annie not pay taxes voluntarily, would be a mighty force. Annie, Bobby, and Callie would pay taxes voluntarily to finance limited services of government.

In a capitalistic society, the Moral Imperative must be the guide star for *all* human interaction, both in the private and the public realm. For all matters that require choice in a social context—the political realm—voting by citizens (democracy) is the only just political institution. As Solon notes, direct democracy in societies larger than a few hundred people has been impractical throughout human history. Consequently, representative government featuring elected legislators, an elected executive, and judges (elected or appointed) has been the accepted alternative in societies that take themselves to be democratic and free.

But representative government is a concession to practicality, a concession that introduces serious problems, if the political institution of majority rule is in play. Representative government creates a small, privileged class of citizens (546 people in the United States—435 Members of Congress, 100 Senators, nine Justices of the Supreme Court, one President, and one chairman of the Federal Reserve). In large societies of millions of people, elected representatives are remote from and mostly inaccessible to most citizens. But sadly enough, elected representatives are *nearby* and *entirely accessible* to the wealthiest members of society. Representative government paves the way for democratic cronyism, a demonstrable outcome that few will deny. In America, K Street in Washington, D.C. is a major portal for special interests and democratic cronyism, as argued persuasively by Mark Grimaldi and Stevenson G. Smith in their book, *Money Compass*.[145]

In a capitalistic society, in which members of society honor the Moral Imperative above all other values, occasions for making positive law will be infrequent. A capitalist society certainly needs a limited body of positive law (mostly for coordination of arbitrary choices that must be made in a social context), certainly needs law enforcement (since some people will disobey just law), certainly needs courts (since interested parties to disputes will be self-interested), and certainly needs executive administration (since specialization and division of labor also increases productivity of government). But all these—legislators, judges, officers of the courts, the executive, and other government operatives—must honor the Moral Imperative in formation, execution, adjudication, and enforcement of law.

Only in political economies *other than capitalism* (e.g., democratic cronyism, military socialism, democratic socialism, democratic fascism, military regime, and strongman dictatorship) is it necessary to create thousands of pages of new positive law each and every year. A truly capitalistic political economy requires very few positive laws.

Adoption of all positive law by voting in a truly capitalistic society would require a super majority—perhaps as high as four-fifths of the citizens or their representatives. Laws that cannot be passed with such a super majority would simply not become law in a truly capitalist society. The popularity and general acceptance of the political institution of majority rule, which is inculcated in most of us in America from childhood, is perhaps based on the soundly discredited philosophy of utilitarianism—the notion of the greatest good for the greatest number. Utilitarianism justifies slavery, if free persons outnumber slaves, which alone is sufficient to condemn the philosophy of utilitarianism to the trash heap of exceptionally bad ideas. Put simply, the political institution of democratic majority rule spawns political economies that are immoral.

Tyro: Solon, history definitely shows us that the principles of capitalism advance human prosperity and freedom more than any other system of political economy. But not everyone is equally well-equipped to prosper in a capitalistic society. In a capitalistic Threesville, won't Callie be poor, since she lacks knowledge, skills, and talents that Annie and Bobby possess?

Solon: Callie will not likely enjoy as much material prosperity in a capitalistic Threesville as Annie and Bobby.

Tyro: That doesn't seem fair.

Solon: Why do you say that, Tyro?

Tyro: Is it Callie's fault that she doesn't have what it takes to become wealthy in a capitalistic Threesville? Didn't she get dealt a bad hand by life?

Solon: That idea seems to be what undergirds the philosophy of John Rawls.

Tyro: Was Rawls wrong to think that way?

Solon: If it is not fair that Callie is less able than Annie and Bobby, would it be fair to compel Annie and Bobby to give goods and services they produce to Callie?

Tyro: I don't see how compulsion of one by another can be fair.

Solon: Nor do I, Tyro. In a capitalistic Threesville, Annie and Bobby are free to help Callie voluntarily, either as individuals or together as a group. If Annie and Bobby are virtuous, they will choose voluntarily to help Callie prosper. History demonstrates amply that moral people tend to be virtuous people and that virtuous people who are prosperous tend to be philanthropic. Why should we think that Callie will suffer in a capitalistic Threesville.

Tyro: Threesville is so small that the society is really like a family, so it wouldn't be surprising if Annie and Bobby will voluntarily help Callie prosper.

Solon: Indeed, Tyro. For us humans, a loving, connected core family is an ideal social unit. Utopians of all kinds—many socialists, for example—have always sought a way to make the larger society like a family. People who yearn for socialism are not usually villains. They are more often people who simply fail to see that only a very small society can be anything like a family. They also fail to see that the socialism they champion will definitely require violation of the Moral Imperative.

Tyro: But what if Annie and Bobby are not particularly virtuous in a capitalistic Threesville? Callie will be poor. Annie will be very rich, and Bobby will be well off. Isn't that outcome objectionable?

Solon: Objectionable for whom?

Tyro: For Callie, of course.

Solon: We would have to ask Callie. Callie might not object to being *relatively* poor. Her quality of life might be pleasant and even agreeable to her in a capitalistic Threesville.

Tyro: No one wants to be poor, Solon.

Solon: No one wants to live in squalor with too little to eat, insufficient shelter, constant danger, and dire prospects for improvement. Is that Callie's condition in a capitalistic Threesville?

Tyro: I don't know. We have not said what being poor is like in a capitalistic Threesville. But what about a society that numbers in the millions like our own?

Solon: Over the most recent 200 years, the quality of life in America has advanced to heights unimaginable in the preceding centuries—heights that allow even the poorest members of our society to live better than all but kings and aristocrats of just 200 years ago.

Tyro: Yes, but what about the rest of the world?

Solon: The quality of life around the globe, though not yet as high as countries of the West, has also advanced spectacularly. Most people in third-word countries today enjoy better health care than the average citizen of America had available in the early 20th Century, believe it or not.[146] I see no reason to doubt that advancing technology, nurtured as it must be by the four principles of capitalism, will continue to advance human prosperity throughout the world.

Tyro: You are an optimist, Solon.

Solon: Perhaps. But I am an optimist based on evidence. History shows us that the poorest members of society prosper *most* in political economies that most closely practice the four principles of true capitalism. That fact is indisputable.

Taking care of the poorest members of society is most advanced and most prevalent in prosperous societies. As it happens, people living in prosperous societies *voluntarily* form charitable associations, a fact of history, demonstrated in middle and late 19th Century America and England.[147] Members of a prosperous society voluntarily form associations to provide care for those in need; they also form associations to provide mutual insurance (e.g., fraternal organizations in America such as Free Masons, Moose Lodge, and many others, not to mention community churches). People living in a prosperous society voluntarily support education—without compulsory taxation (another historical fact demonstrated in early America).[148] No system of political economy promotes prosperous societies like the four principles of capitalism; in fact, no other social system of political economy even comes close. Consequently, nothing promotes care for the less fortunate members of society more than consistent practice of the four principles of capitalism.

Critics of capitalism who favor compulsory taxation and a welfare state argue that people cannot be trusted to take care of those who cannot care for themselves. Such critics evidently have a very low regard for human nature, believing it seems, that only they—the champions of statism and the welfare state—have virtuous and benevolent motives. How very strange, for history is completely clear about the poverty that statism yields. Recent history is also clear about the deficiencies of the welfare state, as demonstrated by the ailing and failing political economies of the so-called PIIGS, Portugal, Italy, Ireland, Greece, and Spain. History is also clear about the philanthropic and charitable associations that arise voluntarily in societies of prosperous people.

Critics of capitalism argue that government must force its citizens, through compulsory taxation, to care for the disadvantaged. Government must force its citizens to pay for what only they—supporters of the overarching state—are able to see is in the "best interest of society." The "free-rider problem," the critics say, requires compulsory taxation and a cradle-to-grave nanny state. But historical evidence does not support those claims.

Even in a large society, social ostracism would play a powerful role to suppress the free-rider problem, notwithstanding the claims of those who say taxes must be mandatory. All that would be required to activate that force is public dissemination of the annual amount of taxes people voluntarily chose to pay in a system of voluntary taxation. Even in America, a society of some 325 million people, Bill Gates would likely find Microsoft products falling out of favor, if he paid taxes substantially below the amount that people think "fair," provided such information were a matter of public record. On the other hand, most people would not object to zero taxes paid voluntarily by Joe the rag man. The rest of us would fall somewhere in between.

Voluntary taxation has the additional merit of limiting activities of government to just those activities that citizens are willing and able to pay for. Without compulsory taxation, the problem of incredible, ever rising sovereign debt all around the globe today would vanish. Few people would buy even U.S. Treasuries (let alone the government bonds of other sovereign states), if they knew that states could not compel payment of taxes. What a pleasant and sensible side effect of a system of voluntary taxation.

Early America had no compulsory income tax. Congress passed an income tax in 1861 to pay for Civil War expenses, but that tax was repealed in 1871. In 1894, Congress passed a flat-rate federal income tax, but the Supreme Court ruled the tax unconstitutional a year later. It was not until 1913 that the states ratified the 16th amendment to the Constitution, passed by Congress in 1909, allowing the federal government to tax income of citizens without regard to population and apportionment among the states.[149] The income tax code of the United States is a prime example of unjust positive law that democracy combined with majority rule produces over time.

In early America, projects believed by some to offer wide-spread benefits were financed through *voluntary subscription* from those who agreed and were able to pay (e.g., a public library and paved streets in Philadelphia, in the days of Benjamin Franklin).[150] Subscribers were not worried about the free-rider problem. They knew that disdain for non-subscribers who were able to pay was a powerful force. Proponents of compulsory taxation and big government typically use the free-rider argument to justify what they take to be "in the public interest." Yet, they have no evidence to support their claims. As an historical matter of fact, in a young America, people who could afford to do so voluntarily paid to finance projects they believed would be beneficial, not just for themselves, but for all in the community. As Michael Novak said, echoing the words of F. A. Hayek,

> *It is one of the greatest weaknesses of our time that we lack the patience and faith to build up voluntary organizations for purposes which we value highly, and (instead) immediately ask the government to bring about by coercion (or with means raised by coercion) anything that appears as desirable to large numbers.*[151]

History shows us that the most prosperous societies in the world are those that most closely and most consistently embrace all four principles of capitalism.[152] History also shows that prosperous societies, such as America, did care for their poor and disadvantaged voluntarily, without compulsory taxation.[153,154,155] People who have great concern for the poor of the world should embrace and champion capitalism.

CAN WE GET THERE FROM HERE?

This book offers and defends two propositions: (1) capitalism is moral and (2) capitalism is the only system of political economy that is moral.

If people want to be moral—and a very large majority of people do—then people should embrace capitalism. We the people should *insist* that our politicians create and enforce a political economy that enshrines and protects all four principles of capitalism. For if we did, we would be insisting on morality in government. Yet, even in America, we live in a political economy that is not true capitalism. Around the world, billions of people live in political economies that are still further removed from capitalism—political economies infested with not just cronyism, but with corruption, self-dealing, and aggressive oppression of the many by the few.

How can we citizens of America insist that we return to the principles of our founding in 1776, which the writers of our Constitution did their best to make the law of the land? Can we get to true capitalism from here? Against all odds, I remain optimistic that we can. I conclude this book with two entirely practical prescriptions that just may offer a way for us to get to true capitalism from here.

The first prescription is for all of us to make a solemn oath (to yourself, for only *you* can hold yourself to an oath) to never, ever vote for an incumbent politician. That's it; really simple. If citizens of America would refuse to vote for incumbents, we would see a splendid and amazing transformation of our political economy—a transformation that would move us closer to true capitalism and away from democratic cronyism.

For decades, each election cycle, voters have returned more than 90% of Members of the House to office. Voters routinely return more than 80% of incumbents to the Senate.[156] A one-term presidency is typically considered a failed presidency. Worse still, Justices of the Supreme Court serve for life or until they choose to retire. Apologists for that highly questionable judicial convention say it is necessary to keep politics out of the deliberations of the Supreme Court—as if that were somehow possible.

The phenomenon of career politicians and judges enables the democratic cronyism that is our political economy in America today. The American political economy is democratic because we get to vote periodically, but the system is highly biased in favor of the power elite and their wealthy petitioners. Lobbyists who inhabit K Street in Washington, D.C. would loose their influence overnight, without career politicians from whom to seek favors. Purveyors of special interest and self-dealing would recognize that the jig is up, if they had to deal with new, fresh citizens in the halls of Congress each and every election cycle. Spending billions in attempts to get self-dealing, positive laws passed (laws that vitiate natural law) would no longer make sense, especially if we also adopted a second prescription.

The second prescription is that we the people refuse to vote for candidates for political office who do not swear to uphold—as a prerequisite for getting on the ballot—the proposition that *all* laws must be passed by a four-fifths majority of the representatives elected to the House and the Senate in America, which representatives would continue to be elected by simple, direct, majority rule, just as they are now. Better still, the four-fifths principle could and should be made an inviolate part of our Constitution by amendment.

It is highly unlikely that special-interest laws—positive laws that empower the few to compel the many—could be passed with a four-fifths majority of representatives who know they will serve but one term. Yet, natural law—and a small body of socially coordinating positive law—could and would be passed with a super majority of four-fifths.

Laws that cannot pass the high hurdle of a four-fifths majority should not be part of the U.S. Code. Moreover, laws that are currently part of the U.S. Code that have not been passed with a four-fifths majority of both houses of Congress should be repealed. If such laws are just laws, they can be and will be reintroduced and passed again by four-fifths of the members of Congress without long delay. After all, the body of law required for true capitalism is not large, so we are not talking about mountains of work for Congress.

If we are unwilling to abolish career politicians (by refusing to vote for incumbents), and if we are unwilling to require a super majority to pass laws, I fear we are unwilling to become a truly capitalist society. If we are unwilling to become a truly capitalist society, we are destined to continue to the end game of the democratic cronyism that is the political economy of America. Unfortunately, that end game features ever expanding control of our lives by the few, ever expanding national debt (more than $17.5 trillion in mid-2014), and a widening gap between the fortunes of the power elite (the 546), their wealthy petitioners (the *real* power elite), and the rest of us.

All societies must somehow answer three fundamental questions in a social context, using the institutions of their political economy: (1) what goods and services to produce using the scarce resources of land, labor, and capital, (2) how to do it, and (3) who gets what is produced.[157] We have only two options for answering those questions. We may *cooperate* with others and *coordinate* our actions with others through *voluntary exchange*, or we may be *compelled* by others to conform to their answers, compelled by the coercive power of government operatives. We cannot do both, for in the fullness of time, one annihilates the other. In all societies at all times throughout history, people have done one or the other. In the end, the two options of voluntary exchange and compulsion become mutually exclusive.

"You, sir, are a dreamer," critics from both the left and the right may say. Perhaps. But it is a worthy dream. Life with true capitalism, founded as it must be on the Moral Imperative, would not be utopian, but it may be the best that we humans can do.

References and Notes

1. Carnegie, Dale (1936). *How to Win Friends and Influence People.* Retrieved 27 March 2012. http://www.google.com/url?sa=t&rct=j&q=&esrc=s&source=web&cd=6&ved=0CHoQFjAF&url=http%3A%2F%2Ferudition.mohit.tripod.com%2F_Influence_People.pdf&ei=ulFyT_39M5C4twfd4NGfCA&usg=AFQjCNE5H9yMB8EwxQSWTsQpS7citqDvYA&sig2=4TadAOIaL2lY1nO7mWdKvQ

2. Smith, Adam. *An Inquiry into the Nature and Causes of the Wealth of Nations.* Edwin Cannan, ed. 1904. Library of Economics and Liberty. Retrieved 27 March 2012. http://www.econlib.org/library/Smith/smWN.html.

3. Bastiat, Claude Frédéric. *Economic Sophisms.* Arthur Goddard, trans. 1996. Library of Economics and Liberty. Retrieved 27 March 2012. http://www.econlib.org/library/Bastiat/basSoph.html.

4. Mises, Ludwig (1949). *Human Action.* Ludwig von Mises Institute. Retrieved 27 March 2012. http://mises.org/page/1470/Human_Action_HTML>

5. Rand, Ayn; Nathaniel Branden; Alan Greenspan; Robert Hessen (1986-07-15). *Capitalism: The Unknown Ideal* (Signet Shakespeare). Penguin Group. Kindle Edition.

6. Friedman, Milton (1962). *Capitalism and Freedom.* University of Chicago Press, Chicago.

7. Hayek, Friedrich (1945). *The Use of Knowledge in Society.* Ludwig von Mises Institute. Retrieved 27 March 2012. < http://mises.org/daily/5615/The-Use-of-Knowledge-in-Society/Use-of-Knowledge-in-Society-The>

8   Kirzner, Israel M. (1976). *The Economic Point of View: An Essay in the History of Economic Thought.* Laurence S. Moss, ed. Library of Economics and Liberty. Retrieved 27 March 2012. http://www.econlib.org/library/NPDBooks/Kirzner/krzPV.html.

9   Reisman, George. (2012-05-19). *Capitalism: A Treatise on Economics* (Kindle Location 2100). TJS Books. Kindle Edition.

10 Rothbard, Murray N. (2004). *Man, Economy, and State.* Ludwig von Mises Institute. Retrieved 27 March 2012. < http://mises.org/rothbard/mes.asp>

11 Johnson, Paul (1990). *First Things.* "The Capitalism and Morality Debates." Retrieved 27 March 2012. http://www.firstthings.com/article/2007/08/003-the-capitalism–morality-debate–1

12 Friedman, Milton (1983). *Bright Promises, Dismal Performance: An Economist's Protest.* Harvest/HBJ Books.

13 Mises, Ludwig (1957). *Theory and History.* Yale University Press.

14 Heyne, Paul, Peter J. Boettke, and David L. Prychitko (2010). *The Economic Way of Thinking.* 12th ed. Prentice Hall.

15 Friedman, Milton (1990). *Free to Choose: A Personal Statement.* Harcourt Brace Jovanovich.

16 Friedman, Milton (2002). *Capitalism and Freedom.* 40th Anniversary Edition. University of Chicago Press.

17 McCloskey, Deidre (1998). *The Rhetoric of Economics.* 2nd Ed. University of Wisconsin Press.

18 Kreeft, Peter (2004). *Ethics: A History of Moral Thought* [Unabridged] [Audible Audio Edition]. The Modern Scholar, Recorded Books, LLC.

19 Kreeft, Peter (1999). *A Refutation Of Moral Relativism: Interviews with an Absolutist* (Kindle Location 2). Ignatius Press. Kindle Edition.

20 Heinlein, Robert (1961). *Stranger in a Strange Land.* Ace Books.

21 Auberon Herbert, 1838 –1906, writer, theorist, philosopher, 19th century individualist, and a member of the Parliament of the United Kingdom. Herbert promoted a libertarian philosophy and advocated voluntarily-funded government that uses force only in defense of individual liberty and property. He is known as the originator of Voluntarism.

22 Carl Sandburg, 1878-1967, American writer and editor, best known for his poetry and his biography of Abraham Lincoln.

23 Allen, Colin. *The Stanford Encyclopedia of Philosophy.* "Animal Consciousness", (Winter 2011 Edition), Edward N. Zalta (ed.), http://plato.stanford.edu/archives/win2011/entries/consciousness-animal

24 *Online Etymology Dictionary.* Retrieved 12 June 2013. http://etymonline.com/index.php?term=sentient&allowed_in_frame=0

25 Rideout, N. Kenneth (2005). *The Truth You Know You Know.* NDX Press.

26 *Project Gutenberg.* Retrieved 25 June 2012. http://www.gutenberg.org/browse/authors/a

27 Klein, Daniel and Thomas Cathcart (2008-06-24). *Plato and a Platypus Walk into a Bar: Understanding Philosophy Through Jokes* (pp. 85-86). Penguin Group. Kindle Edition

28 *Brainy Quote*. Retrieved 25 June 2012. http://www.brainyquote.com/quotes/quotes/g/georgebern109537.html

29 Kant, Immanuel (2004-05-01). *Fundamental Principles of the Metaphysic of Morals*. Thomas Kingsmill Abbott (trans.). Public Domain Books. Kindle Edition.

30 Kant, Immanuel [1785] (1993). *Grounding for the Metaphysics of Morals*. 3rd ed., translated by James W. Ellington Hackett. Hackett Publishing Company, Inc. pp. 30.

31 *Stanford Encyclopedia of Philosophy*. "Ethics-virtue," Retrieved 10 May 2012. http://plato.stanford.edu/entries/ethics-virtue/

32 Mill, John Stuart (1863). *Utilitarianism*. Project Gutenberg. Retrieved 10 July 2012. http://www.gutenberg.org/ebooks/11224

33 *Online Etymology Dictionary*. Retrieved 7 August 2012. http://www.etymonline.com/

34 Fletcher, Joseph (1966). *Situation Ethics*. Westminster John Knox Press.

35 Rawls, John (1971). *A Theory of Justice*. Belknap Press.

36 Nozick, Robert (1974-09-01). *Anarchy, State, And Utopia*. Basic Books. Kindle Edition.

37 *Wise Old Sayings*. "Quotes." Retrieved 20 July 2012. http://www.wiseoldsayings.com/wosdirectoryo.htm

38 According to the Greek writer Pausanias, this phrase was inscribed on the Temple of Apollo at Delphi. Pausanias was a Greek traveler and geographer of the 2nd century AD, who lived in the times of Hadrian, Antoninus Pius and Marcus Aurelius.

39 Aquinas, St. Thomas. *Summa Theologica.* Retrieved 17 May 2012. http://en.wikisource.org/wiki/Summa_Theologiae/First_Part_of_the_Second_Part

40 Ayn Rand was a Russian-American novelist, philosopher, playwright, and screenwriter. She is known for her two best-selling novels *The Fountainhead* and *Atlas Shrugged.* She developed a philosophy called objectivism.

41 Mises, Ludwig von (1949, 1998). *Human Action.* The Scholars Edition. Ludwig von Mises Institute. p. 11.

42 Aquinas, St. Thomas (1275). *Summa Theologica. Prima Secundae Partis, Question 1.* Benziger Bros. edition, (1947) Translated by Fathers of the English Dominican Province.

43 Ross, David (1925). Aristotle The Nicomachean Ethics: Translated with an Introduction. Oxford: Oxford University Press. Re-issued 1980, revised by J. L. Ackrill and J. O. Urmson.

44 Daniel N. Robinson. (1999). *Aristotle's Psychology.* Published by Daniel N. Robinson.

45 Kreeft, Peter. *Back to Virtue.* Google Books. Retrieved 19 July 2012. http://books.google.com/books?id=55QdKe3FmYMC&pg=PA130&lpg=PA130&dq=rabbi+abraham+heschel+suffer&source=bl&ots=qej7C3pBDx&sig=QNbWRbVedjxrdTgp0JrFNtPVQ0I&hl=en&sa=X&ei=zJMIUI79JIbs0gH45L3WAw&ved=0CGIQ

6AEwBTgy#v=onepage&q=rabbi%20abraham%20heschel%20suffer&f=false

46 Ross, David (1925). *Aristotle The Nicomachean Ethics: Translated with an Introduction.* Oxford: Oxford University Press. Re-issued 1980, revised by J. L. Ackrill and J. O. Urmson.

47 Socrates (c. 469 BC – 399 BC), was a classical Greek Athenian philosopher, the principle figure in the dialogues of Plato.

48 Aristotle (384 BC – 322 BC), perhaps the most celebrated Greek, a longtime student of Plato.

49 Descartes, René (1641). *Meditations on First Philosophy.* The Philosophical Writings of René Descartes, trans. by J. Cottingham, R. Stoothoff and D. Murdoch, Cambridge: Cambridge University Press, 1984.

50 Reid, Thomas. *Early Modern Texts.* "Essays on the Intellectual Powers of Man." Retrieved 13 July 2012. http://www.earlymoderntexts.com/pdfbits/reip.html

51 Sartre, Jean-Paul. *Existentialism Is a Humanism* (translated by Carol Macomber, introduction by Annie Cohen-Solal, notes and preface by Arlette Elkaïm-Sartre) Yale University Press, New Haven, 2007, p. 10.

52 Albert Einstein (1879 –1955), the father of modern physics, German theoretical physicist who developed the theory of general relativity.

53 Gottfried Wilhelm Leibniz (1646 –1716), German mathematician and philosopher.

54 Henry Louis "H. L." Mencken (1880 - 1956), American journalist, essayist, magazine editor, satirist, critic of American life and culture, and a scholar of American English.

55 Fine, G. (2003). *Plato on Knowledge and Forms: Selected Essays.* Introduction. Oxford University Press,), p. 5.

56 Descartes, René; Laurence J. Lafleur (trans.) (1960). *Discourse on Method and Meditations.* New York: The Liberal Arts Press.

57 Quine, W.V.O. (1970). *Philosophy of Logic.* Prentice-Hall.

58 Kant, Immanuel. (1781/1998). *The Critique of Pure Reason.* Trans. by P. Guyer and A.W. Wood, Cambridge University Press.

59 Kant, Immanuel. (1781/1998). *The Critique of Pure Reason.* Trans. by P. Guyer and A.W. Wood, Cambridge University Press.

60 Ayer, A. J. (1936, 1952). *Language, Truth and Logic.* New York: Dover Publications.

61 Aquinas, St. Thomas. *Summa Theologica.* Retrieved 17 May 2012. http://en.wikisource.org/wiki/Summa_Theologiae/First_Part/Question_1

62 *Quotationsbook.* Retrieved 3 May 2012. http://quotationsbook.com/quote/14040/

63 McGinn, Colin. *Learnoutloud.* Retrieved 3 May 2012. http://www.learnoutloud.com/Audio-Books/Philosophy/Ancient-and-Medieval-Philosophy/Discovering-the-Philosopher-in-You/3489

64 *Internet Encyclopedia of Philosophy.* "Protagoras." Retrieved 5 June 2012. http://www.iep.utm.edu/protagor/

65 Coxon A. H. (2009). *The Fragments of Parmenides: A Critical Text With Introduction and Translation, the Ancient Testimonia and a Commentary.* Las Vegas, Parmenides Publishing (new edition of Coxon 1986).

66 *The Oxford Dictionary of World Religions.* ed. John Bowke, Oxford University Press. 1997

67 Hobbes, Thomas. (1651). *Leviathan.* Kindle Edition. (Kindle Location 2059).

68 Hobbes, Thomas. (1651). *Leviathan.* Kindle Edition. (Kindle Location 2042)

69 *Acton Institute.* Retrieved 22 August 2012. http://www.acton.org/research/lord-acton

70 *Constitution.* Madison, James. "*The Federalist No. 51.*" Retrieved 7 August 2012. http://www.constitution.org/fed/federa51.htm

71 Rawls, John (1971). *A Theory of Justice.* Belknap Press: Cambridge, MA.

72 Styron, William. (1979). *Sophie's Choice.* Random House. New York.

73 *Listverse.* "Top 10 Moral Dilemmas." Retrieved 19 August 2012. http://listverse.com/2007/10/21/top-10-moral-dilemmas/

74 Lovett, Frank. (2011). *Rawl's Theory of Justice: A Reader's Guide.* Kindle Edition.

References and Notes

75 *Stanford Encyclopedia of Philosophy.* "Moral Dilemmas." Retrieved 10 August 2012. http://plato.stanford.edu/entries/moral-dilemmas/

76 Henry David Thoreau (1817 –1862), American author, poet, philosopher, naturalist, and historian.

77 Kant, Immanuel. *Groundwork for the Metaphysics of Morals.* Google Books. Retrieved 1 September 2012. http://books.google.com/books?id=YASbAEhCLw0C&pg=PA105&lpg=PA105&dq=We+have+finally+reduced+the+definite+conception+of+morality+to+the+idea+of+freedom.&source=bl&ots=rxJ9Nkj7FT&sig=9b_ZytRBScC4MrqRi6gW3TSW0Ls&hl=en#v=onepage&q=We%20have%20finally%20reduced%20the%20definite%20conception%20of%20morality%20to%20the%20idea%20of%20freedom.&f=false. p. 105.

78 *Library of Economics and Liberty.* Smith, Adam (1776). "An Inquiry into the Nature and Causes of the Wealth of Nations."Edwin Cannan, ed. 1904. Retrieved 27 March 2012. http://www.econlib.org/library/Smith/smWN.html

79 Mises, Ludwig von. 1957. *Theory and History.* Yale University Press.

80 Hume, David. (2011-03-24). *A Treatise of Human Nature,* (1739-40), Book III, Part 1, Section 1. Kindle Edition.

81 Ayn Rand (1906-1982), Russian-American novelist, philosopher, playwright, and screenwriter. She is known for her two best-selling novels, The Fountainhead and Atlas Shrugged, and for her philosophy, which is called objectivism.

82 Kenneth Robert Minogue (1930-), Australian political theorist, Emeritus Professor of Political Science and Honorary Fellow at the London School of Economics.

83 Rand, Ayn; Nathaniel Branden; Alan Greenspan; Robert Hessen (1986-07-15). *Capitalism: The Unknown Ideal* (Signet Shakespeare) (p. 10). Penguin Group. Kindle Edition.

84 Milton Friedman. *Capitalism and Freedom: Fortieth Anniversary Edition* (Kindle Location 262). Kindle Edition.

85 *Google.* Capitalism. Retrieved 17 October 2012. https://www.google.com/search?q=capitalism&ie=utf-8&oe=utf-8&aq=t&rls=org.mozilla:en-US:official&client=firefox-a.

86 Sadowsky, James. (1966). *Private Property and Collective Ownership.* Retrieved 30 November 2012. http://www.quebecoislibre.org/030607-3.htm.

87 Locke, John (2009-06-19). *Two Treatises of Government* (p. 12). MacMay. Kindle Edition.

88 Locke, John (2009-06-19). *Two Treatises of Government* (p. 12). MacMay. Kindle Edition.

89 Rothbard, Murray. *The Ethics of Liberty.* Ludwig Von Mises Institute. Retrieved 28 October 2013. http://mises.org/Literature/Author/299/Murray-N-Rothbard

90 Marx, Karl. *Critique of the Gotha Program.* Retrieved 30 October 2012. http://www.marxists.org/archive/marx/works/1875/gotha/

91 Rothbard, Murray N. (1962). *Man, Economy & State with Power and Market.* Ludwig von Mises Institute ISBN 978-0-945466-30-7 Ch. 2. Retrieved 3 November 2012. http://mises.org/document/1082/Man-Economy-and-State-with-Power-and-Market

92 Rothbard, Murray N. (1962). *Man, Economy & State with Power and Market*. Ludwig von Mises Institute ISBN 978-0-945466-30-7 Ch. 2. Retrieved 3 November 2012. http://mises.org/document/1082/Man-Economy-and-State-with-Power-and-Market

93 Nozick, Robert (1974-09-01). *Anarchy, State, And Utopia* (p. 174). Basic Books. Kindle Edition.

94 Nozick, Robert (1974-09-01). Anarchy, State, And Utopia (p. 178). Basic Books. Kindle Edition.

95 de Jasay, Anthony (1997). *Against Politics : On Government, Anarchy, and Order* (1. publ. ed.). London [u.a.]: Routledge. pp. 173.

96 Hoppe, Hans-Hermann (2006). *The Economics and Ethics of Private Property : Studies in Political Economy and Philosophy* (2nd ed.). Auburn, Ala. Ludwig von Mises Institute. pp. 199.

97 George, Henry (1879). *Progress and Poverty: An Inquiry into the Cause of Industrial Depressions and of Increase of Want with Increase of Wealth*. Retrieved 5 November 2012. http://www.econlib.org/library/YPDBooks/George/grgPP.html

98 Rothbard, Murray N. (1962). *Man, Economy & State with Power and Market*. Ludwig von Mises Institute ISBN 978-0-945466-30-7 Ch. 2. Retrieved 3 November 2012. http://mises.org/document/1082/Man-Economy-and-State-with-Power-and-Market

99 Mises, Ludwig von. *Human Action*. Retrieved 14 December 2013. http://mises.org/humanaction/chap15sec3.asp#[7]

100 Nozick, Robert (1974-09-01). *Anarchy, State, And Utopia* (p. 160). Perseus Book Group-A. Kindle Edition.

101 Nozick, Robert (1974-09-01). *Anarchy, State, And Utopia* (p. 160). Perseus Book Group-A. Kindle Edition.

102 Mises, Ludwig von. *Human Action*. Retrieved 14 December 2013. http://mises.org/humanaction

103 Friedman, Milton. *Capitalism and Freedom: Fortieth Anniversary Edition*. Kindle Edition.

104 Rothbard, Murray. *It All Began As Usual With the Greeks*. Retrieved 25 June 2013. http://mises.org/daily/2054

105 Hardin, Garrett. *Tragedy of the Commons*. Retrieved 9 July 2013, http://www.econlib.org/library/Enc/TragedyoftheCommons.html

106 Smith, Adam (2011-04-29). *The Wealth of Nations (Illustrated)* (p. 11). Kindle Edition.

107 Ricardo, David. 1817. *On the Principles of Political Economy and Taxation*. In The Works and Correspondence of David Ricardo. 11 vols. Edited by Piero Sraffa, with the collaboration of M. H. Dobb. Cambridge: Cambridge University Press, 1951–1973. Retrieved 9 July 2013. http://www.econlib.org/library/Ricardo/ricP.html

108 Smith, Adam (2011-04-29). *The Wealth of Nations (Illustrated)*. (p. 11). Kindle Edition.

109 Read, Leonard E. *I, Pencil*. Retrieved 1 July 2013 http://www.econlib.org/library/Essays/rdPncl1.html

110 Nozick, Robert (1974-09-01). *Anarchy, State, And Utopia* (pp. 263-264). Basic Books. Kindle Edition.

111 Nozick, Robert (1974-09-01). *Anarchy, State, And Utopia* (p. 262). Basic Books. Kindle Edition.

112 Nozick, Robert (1974-09-01). *Anarchy, State, And Utopia* (p. 263). Basic Books. Kindle Edition.

113 Smith, Adam (2011-04-29). *The Wealth of Nations (Illustrated)*. (pp. 11-12). Kindle Edition.

114 Rawls, John (1971). *A Theory of Justice*. Belknap Press: Cambridge, MA.

115 Rousseau, Jean-Jacques. (1762). *Du Contrat Social ou Principes du Doit Politique*. Retrieved 3 July 2013. http://www.constitution.org/jjr/socon.htm

116 Claude Frédéric Bastiat (1801– 1850) was a French classical liberal theorist, political economist, and member of the French assembly.

117 Hobbes, Thomas (1651). *Leviathan*. (Kindle Location 2042)

118 Aquinas, St. Thomas (1275). *Summa Theologica. Prima Secundae Partis, Question 94*. Benziger Bros. edition, (1947) Translated by Fathers of the English Dominican Province.

119 Tannehill, Morris and Linda. *The Market for Liberty*. Retrieved 26 July 2013. http://mises.org/document/6058/The-Market-for-Liberty

120 Bastiat, Frederick (2008-06-01). *The Law*. (p. 14). Misbach Enterprises. Kindle Edition.

121 Bastiat, Frederick (2008-06-01). *The Law*. (p. 48). Misbach Enterprises. Kindle Edition.

References and Notes

122 Bastiat, Frederick (2008-06-01). *The Law.* (p. 5). Misbach Enterprises. Kindle Edition.

123 Bastiat, Frederick (2008-06-01). *The Law.* (p. 20). Misbach Enterprises. Kindle Edition.

124 Bastiat, Frederick (2008-06-01). *The Law.* (p. 20). Misbach Enterprises. Kindle Edition.

125 Ronald Ernest "Ron" Paul (1935-) American physician, author, and former politician who served multiple terms as the U.S. Representative for Texas.

126 Johnson, Paul (1990). *First Things.* "The Capitalism and Morality Debates." 27 March 2012. http://www.firstthings.com/article/2007/08/003-the-capitalism–morality-debate–1

127 Friedman, Milton (1983). *Bright Promises, Dismal Performance: An Economist's Protest.* Harvest/HBJ Books.

128 *2013 Index of Economic Freedom.* Retrieved 30 November 2013. http://www.heritage.org/index/ranking

129 "Black Faces in Limousines:" A Conversation with Noam Chomsky. Retrieved March 4, 2014. http://www.chomsky.info/interviews/20081114.htm

130 Lewis, Hunter (2013-09-01). *Crony Capitalism in America: 2008-2012.* AC2 Books. Kindle Edition.

131 Rand, Ayn; Nathaniel Branden; Alan Greenspan; Robert Hessen (1986-07-15). *Capitalism: The Unknown Ideal.* Signet Shakespeare. Kindle Locations 33-34. Penguin Group. Kindle Edition.

132 Mises, Ludwig von. *Human Action*. Retrieved 14 December 2013. http://mises.org/humanaction

133 Walter Williams (1936 -) American economist, commentator, and academic. He is the John M. Olin Distinguished Professor of Economics at George Mason University, as well as a syndicated columnists and author.

134 Plato (2009-10-04). *The Republic*. (Kindle Locations 4919-4920). Public Domain Books. Kindle Edition

135 Popper, Karl (1950). *The Open Society and Its Enemies*, Vol. 1: The Spell of Plato, New York: Routledge.

136 Smith, Adam. *An Inquiry into the Nature and Causes of the Wealth of Nations*. Edwin Cannan, ed. 1904. Library of Economics and Liberty. 27 March 2012.

137 Mises, Ludwig von. 1957. *Theory and History*. Yale University Press.

138 Mises, Ludwig von. 1957. *Theory and History*. Yale University Press.

139 Rawls, John (1971). *A Theory of Justice*. Belknap Press.

140 Landsburg, Steven E. (2012). *The Greatest Story Ever Told*. Retrieved March 4, http://www.thebigquestions.com/videos/cato1.html

141 Landsburg, Steven. *The Wall Street Journal*. "A Brief History of Economic Time." (New York, NY). June 9, 2007.

142 Proudhon, P.J. *General Idea of the Revolution in the Nineteenth Century*. trans. John Beverly Robinson (London: Freedom Press, 1923), pp. 293-294, with some alterations from Benjamin Tucker's translation

in Instead of a Book (New York, 1893), p. 26. In Nozick, Robert (1974-09-01). *Anarchy, State, And Utopia* (p. 369). Basic Books. Kindle Edition.

143 Heinlein, Robert A. (1966). *The Moon Is A Harsh Mistress.* Tom Doherty Associates, Inc. New York. p. 82.

144 Nozick, Robert (1974-09-01). *Anarchy, State, And Utopia.* Location 6855. Basic Books. Kindle Edition.

145 Grimaldi, Mark and Stevenson G. Smith (2013-12-17). *The Money Compass: Where Your Money Went and How to Get It Back.* Wiley. Kindle Edition.

146 Landsburg, Steven E. (2012). *The Greatest Story Ever Told.* Retrieved March 4, 2014. http://www.thebigquestions.com/videos/cato1.html

147 Friedman, Milton. *Capitalism and Freedom: Fortieth Anniversary Edition* (Kindle Locations 2373-2374). Kindle Edition.

148 Peterson, Robert A. *The Freeman.* "Education in Colonial America." Retrieved May 6, 2014. http://www.fee.org/the_freeman/detail/education-in-colonial-america

149 *IRS History.* Retrieved May 7, 2014. http://www.loc.gov/rr/business/-hottopic/irs_history.html

150 Benjamin, Franklin. Vook (2010-12-28). *The Autobiography of Benjamin Franklin* (p. 82). Vook. Kindle Edition.

151 Novak, Michael. *First Things.* "Defining Social Justice." Retrieved March 27, 2014. http://www.firstthings.com/article/2007/01/defining-social-justice-29

References and Notes

152 Friedman, Milton (1962). *Capitalism and Freedom.* University of Chicago Press, Chicago.

153 *National Philanthropic Trust.* Retrieved May 7, 2014. http://www.nptrust.org/history-of-giving/philanthropic-quotes/

154 Bremner, Robert H (1988). *American Philanthropy.* 2nd Edition. University of Chicago Press.

155 Zunz, Olivier (2012). *Philanthropy in America: A History.* Princeton University Press.

156 *Open Secrets.* Retrieved March 29, 2014. https://www.opensecrets.org/bigpicture/reelect.php

157 Friedman, Milton. *Capitalism and Freedom: Fortieth Anniversary Edition.* (Kindle Locations 259-260). Kindle Edition.